ASCENT®
CENTER FOR TECHNICAL KNOWLEDGE

Autodesk® Inventor® 2018
Working with 3D Annotations &
Model-Based Definition

Learning Guide
Mixed Units - 1st Edition

AUTODESK.
Authorized Publisher

ASCENT - Center for Technical Knowledge®
Autodesk® Inventor® 2018
Working with 3D Annotations & Model-Based Definition
Mixed Units - 1st Edition

Prepared and produced by:

ASCENT Center for Technical Knowledge
630 Peter Jefferson Parkway, Suite 175
Charlottesville, VA 22911

866-527-2368
www.ASCENTed.com

Lead Contributor: Jennifer MacMillan

ASCENT - Center for Technical Knowledge is a division of Rand Worldwide, Inc., providing custom developed knowledge products and services for leading engineering software applications. ASCENT is focused on specializing in the creation of education programs that incorporate the best of classroom learning and technology-based training offerings.

We welcome any comments you may have regarding this learning guide, or any of our products. To contact us please email: feedback@ASCENTed.com.

Contents

Preface

Autodesk® Inventor® 2018: Working with 3D Annotations & Model-Based Definition teaches experienced Autodesk Inventor users how to create 3D annotations to support the visual presentation of annotations in 3D PDF format and a Model-based Definition (MBD) workflow.

The geometry designed in a 3D CAD modeling environment is created perfectly. During the manufacturing stage, it is not possible to achieve the same perfection. Variations in size, feature location, and orientation are unavoidable. This learning guide instructs how to use the tools in Autodesk Inventor 2018 to create 3D annotations that communicate dimensional and GD&T data, hold/thread notes, surface texture requirements, and informational text-based annotations; all of which aim to improve manufacturing accuracy. Additionally, this learning guide explains how you can share your 3D annotated models as 3D PDFs, as STEP files for use by other software applications, or in 2D drawing views.

Knowledge of GD&T required.

The international GD&T standard, ASME Y14.5M-1994, governs how annotations should be added to clearly describe the model's intent. This learning guide assumes that you know how the model is to be annotated and aims to only explain how they are added using the Autodesk Inventor software.

Topics Covered

- Creating dimensional annotations.

- Creating hole/thread note annotations.

- Creating surface texture annotations.

- Creating text-based annotations to a model to communicate additional modeling information.

- Creating tolerance features to a model.

- Using the Tolerance Advisor to review informational messages and warnings on the tolerance features in a model.

- Creating a general profile note annotation.

- Editing 3D annotations in a model.

- Working with Design Views to accurately present the 3D annotations.

- Exporting an annotated model as 3D PDF or STEP 242 files.

- Retrieving 3D model annotations into a 2D drawing view.

Note on Software Setup

This learning guide assumes a standard installation of the software using the default preferences during installation. Lectures and practices use the standard software templates and default options for the Content Libraries.

Students and Educators can Access Free Autodesk Software and Resources

Autodesk challenges you to get started with free educational licenses for professional software and creativity apps used by millions of architects, engineers, designers, and hobbyists today. Bring Autodesk software into your classroom, studio, or workshop to learn, teach, and explore real-world design challenges the way professionals do.

Get started today - register at the Autodesk Education Community and download one of the many Autodesk software applications available.

Visit www.autodesk.com/joinedu/

Note: Free products are subject to the terms and conditions of the end-user license and services agreement that accompanies the software. The software is for personal use for education purposes and is not intended for classroom or lab use.

Lead Contributor: Jennifer MacMillan

With a dedication for engineering and education, Jennifer has spent over 20 years at ASCENT managing courseware development for various CAD products. Trained in Instructional Design, Jennifer uses her skills to develop instructor-led and web-based training products as well as knowledge profiling tools.

Jennifer has achieved the Autodesk Certified Professional certification for Inventor and is also recognized as an Autodesk Certified Instructor (ACI). She enjoys teaching the training courses that she authors and is also very skilled in providing technical support to end-users.

Jennifer holds a Bachelor of Engineering Degree as well as a Bachelor of Science in Mathematics from Dalhousie University, Nova Scotia, Canada.

Jennifer MacMillan has been the Lead Contributor for *Autodesk Inventor Working with 3D Annotations & Model-Based Definition* since its initial release in 2017.

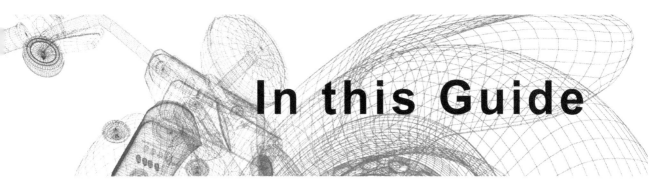

In this Guide

The following images highlight some of the features that can be found in this Learning Guide.

FTP link for practice files

Practice Files

The Practice Files page tells you how to download and install the practice files that are provided with this learning guide.

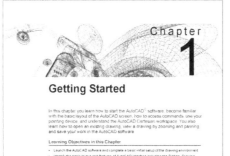

Learning Objectives for the chapter

Chapters

Each chapter begins with a brief introduction and a list of the chapter's Learning Objectives.

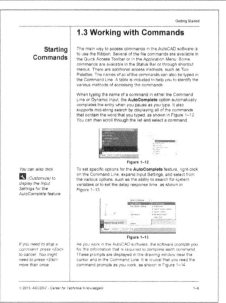

Instructional Content

Each chapter is split into a series of sections of instructional content on specific topics. These lectures include the descriptions, step-by-step procedures, figures, hints, and information you need to achieve the chapter's Learning Objectives.

Side notes

Side notes are hints or additional information for the current topic.

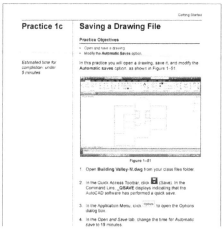

Practice Objectives

Practices

Practices enable you to use the software to perform a hands-on review of a topic.

Some practices require you to use prepared practice files, which can be downloaded from the link found on the Practice Files page.

Chapter Review Questions

Chapter review questions, located at the end of each chapter, enable you to review the key concepts and learning objectives of the chapter.

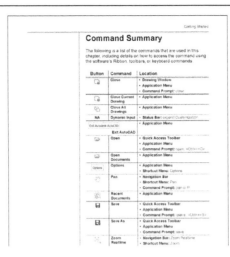

Command Summary

The Command Summary is located at the end of each chapter. It contains a list of the software commands that are used throughout the chapter, and provides information on where the command is found in the software.

Practice Files

To download the practice files for this learning guide, use the following steps:

1. Type the URL shown below into the address bar of your Internet browser. The URL must be typed **exactly as shown**. If you are using an ASCENT ebook, you can click on the link to download the file.

Address bar

http://www.ascented.com/getfile?id=apaturairis

File   Edit   View   Favorites   Tools   Help

2. Press <Enter> to download the .ZIP file that contains the Practice Files.

3. Once the download is complete, unzip the file to a local folder. The unzipped file contains an .EXE file.

4. Double-click on the .EXE file and follow the instructions to automatically install the Practice Files on the C:\ drive of your computer.

   Do not change the location in which the Practice Files folder is installed. Doing so can cause errors when completing the practices in this learning guide.

http://www.ascented.com/getfile?id=apaturairis

Stay Informed!

Interested in receiving information about upcoming promotional offers, educational events, invitations to complimentary webcasts, and discounts? If so, please visit:

www.ASCENTed.com/updates/

Help us improve our product by completing the following survey:

www.ASCENTed.com/feedback

You can also contact us at: *feedback@ASCENTed.com*

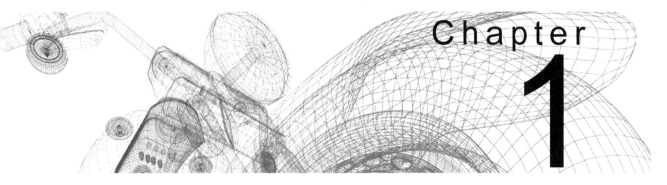

Chapter
1

3D Annotations in Autodesk Inventor

This chapter introduces the concept of 3D annotations. It teaches you how to use the Annotation tools available in the Autodesk® Inventor® software to support the visual presentation of annotations in 3D PDF format, and how to use annotations to support a Model-based Definition (MBD) workflow.

Learning Objectives in this Chapter

- Describe how 3D annotations are used in a model to help visualize the design in a 3D configuration as opposed to a 2D drawing.
- Describe MBD and how adding 3D annotations to a model supports sharing data that is machine readable, enabling software applications to directly use the data.
- Navigate to and access the available annotation tools to review, edit, and create 3D annotations.
- Review the current active standard used in the part model when 3D annotations are added.

1.1 Introduction to Annotations

The ability to create annotations directly in a 3D model was implemented with the release of Autodesk Inventor 2018. The available tools enable you to incorporate and display valuable manufacturing information directly on the 3D model. The new Annotation functionality supports:

Once annotated, a 3D model should be able to replace the requirement for 2D drawings.

• The creation and display of 3D annotations that can be shared and viewed for visual purposes using a 3D PDF.

• The Model-based Definition (MBD) process for annotating a 3D model with the required design data for manufacturing. The export file (STEP 242) produces a machine readable file that enables software applications and CNC tools to directly use the data.

Figure 1–1 shows an example of an annotated 3D model.

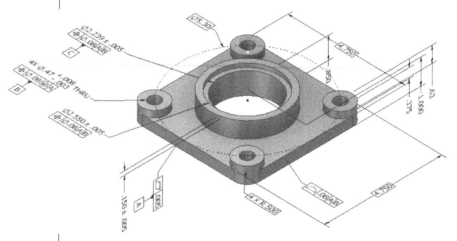

Figure 1–1

Prior to adding 3D annotations, consider the following:

• Use appropriate dimensions and tolerances when creating the model geometry. Sketch and feature dimensions can be promoted and used as 3D annotations to reduce the need for creating new dimensions.

• Know the intent of the model and, if required, how it will interact with any top level assembly files. This understanding will help when creating GD&T annotations.

1.2 General MBD Overview

The PMI data stored in a model is the data that supports MBE. Functionality on the Annotation tab in Autodesk Inventor provides the tools to create the PMI data using an MBD workflow.

Model-based Definition (MBD) is an industry term that refers to the process of creating all design information required to fully and accurately describe a 3D model within its design file. The annotations added to the 3D model supplement the parametric modeling data to fully define how the model is to be manufactured. By including all manufacturing information in the design file, the need for a 2D drawing is eliminated.

The following terms are commonly used when discussing MBD:

- *Product Manufacturing Information* (PMI): The annotations and attribute data included along with the parametric modeling data to create the digital data set.

- *Model-based Engineering (*MBE): The modeling strategy that produces a single master file containing all of a model's 3D design data.

Design Methodologies

An early design and documentation method uses a single file, a 2D Drawing, to show the part definition and geometric dimensioning & tolerancing information (GD&T) that is required to manufacture a model. Figure 1–2 shows a drawing containing dimensions and geometric tolerancing information.

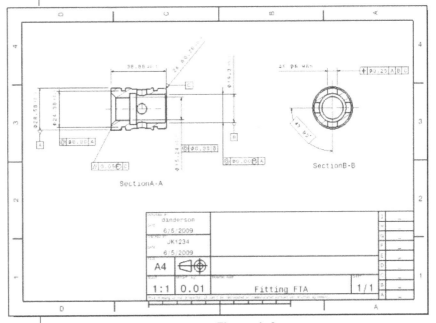

Figure 1–2

Another earlier method, which is still commonly used today, is the two file system. In this method, a 3D file contains the model geometry and the 2D file contains the views, annotations, dimensions, and GD&T data, as shown in Figure 1–3.

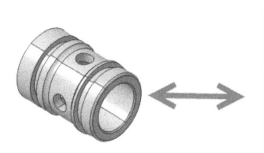
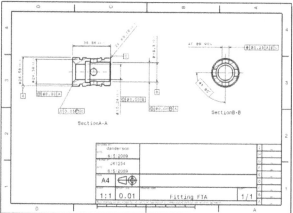

Figure 1–3

Present and Future Methods

The Automotive, Aerospace, Heavy Equipment, Military/Defense, Medical Devices, Electronics, and Consumer Products industries are some of the industries implementing an MBE modeling environment.

Today, using an MBD workflow in an MBE modeling environment produces a single master file that contains all of a model's 3D design data, as well as the PMI information required to manufacture it. MBE is being implemented in many industries to help get better products to market faster, with fewer costly errors. Benefits include the following:

- MBE reduces duplication of effort and prevents contradictory information from occurring between the 3D model and the 2D drawing. Ultimately, it can lead to paperless documentation.

- MBE reduces the amount of data created, stored, and tracked. Additionally, Product Lifecycle Management (PLM) is simplified by only having to manage a single file.

- Quality Control and Part Inspection information is easily relayed.

- MBE easily adapts to the First Article Inspection (FAI) process. This is the process of inspecting a manufactured part to the required GD&T data and then producing a documented report for quality control purposes.

- MBE provides for collaboration across an entire business: Engineering/Design, Manufacturing, Quality Control & Inspection, Project Management, etc., as shown in Figure 1–4. All of these groups (as shown in) can easily view their required data.

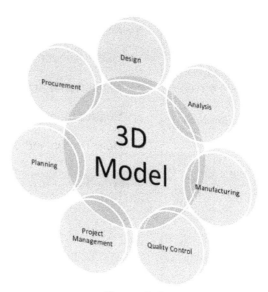

Figure 1–4

Governing Standard:

The American Society of Mechanical Engineer standard Y14.41 (ASME Y14.41) defines the requirements for Model-based Definition in a CAD software and for users creating products using 3D modeling tools.

1.3 The Annotate Interface

To add 3D annotations to an Autodesk Inventor part model, you can use the tools available in the *Annotate* tab. These tools (shown in Figure 1–5) enable you to create the following annotations to support both the inclusion of 3D annotations for visual purposes and an MBD workflow:

- GD&T Annotations (Tolerance Features)

- Dimensional Annotations

- Surface Texture Annotations

- Hole/Thread and General Notes

The annotation tools can only be accessed in the ribbon. There are no context menu options available to initiate their creation.

Figure 1–5

Model Browser

As 3D annotations are added to the model, they are listed in one of two folders that are automatically added to the Model Browser. These folders (shown in Figure 1–6) divide the dimensional, hole/thread, surface, and note based annotations into the **Annotations** folder, and the GD&T annotations into the **Tolerance Features** folder.

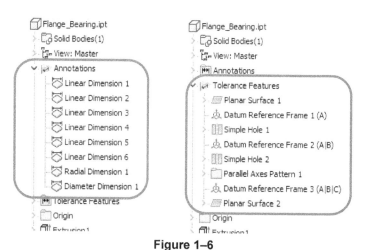

Figure 1–6

Context Menus

There are context menus available when right-clicking on any annotation or tolerance features in the Model Browser. Alternatively, similar context menus are available by right-clicking on an annotation in the graphics window. These menus provide access to additional options that can help place/orient the annotation, set the precision, add text, control its visibility, etc. Figure 1–7 shows the context menus available for radial dimension annotations.

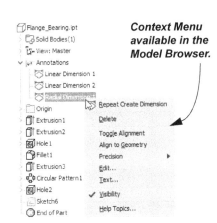

Context Menu available in the Model Browser.

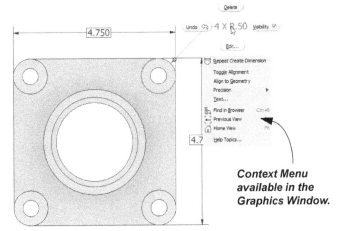

Context Menu available in the Graphics Window.

Figure 1–7

Annotation Selection

*The **Select Annotations** selection priority can also be set in the graphics window by pressing and holding the <Shift> key with the right mouse button (RMB).*

Any 3D annotation can be selected in the graphics window or in the appropriate folder in the Model Browser. When selected in one location, it also highlights in the other to help identify it.

- Annotations can be selected when the **Select Faces and Edges** selection priority is set. Press and hold <Ctrl> or <Shift> to select multiple annotations at once.

- Use the **Select Annotations** selection priority in the Quick Access toolbar (shown in Figure 1–8) to enable annotation selection only. This also enables you to use the window selection method to select multiple annotations at once.

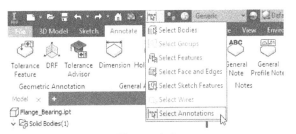

Figure 1–8

1.4 Active Standard

The Active Standard must be set in each file prior to adding any MBD annotations. This standard defines the units of measure that will be used when annotating the 3D model and the GD&T standards. If the model was created with a 2018 default template, the active style is preset; however, if the model was created in any pre-2018 software release, you must assign the active standard before adding any 3D annotations.

The two options for setting this standard in pre-2018 models are:

- In the *Tools* tab>Options panel, click 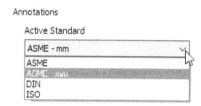 (Document Settings). In the Document Settings dialog box, select the *Standard* tab and select an Active Standard from the drop-down list, as shown in Figure 1–9.

*The default setting for a model created with the 2018 Metric part standard template is **ASME-mm**. The default setting for a model created with the 2018 Imperial part standard template is **ASME**.*

Figure 1–9

- As soon as you access any commands in the *Annotate* tab, you are immediately prompted (as shown in Figure 1–10) to specify the annotation standard that will be used for the part document. Select the standard from the drop-down list and click **OK**.

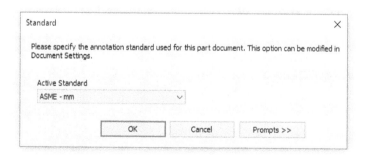

Figure 1–10

Once annotations are added in the model, you can return to the Document Settings dialog box to change the annotation standard, if required. If changing from an *ASME* to an **ISO** or **DIN** standard, you are prompted with the Tolerance Standard Mismatch dialog box, as shown in Figure 1–11. This requires you to select whether to delete mismatched model annotations or not.

Figure 1–11

TIP: 3D Annotation Color

The active color scheme set for the software controls the color of any created annotations and the selection color when they are selected or modified.

Supported Environments

The *Annotation* tab and its tools are only available in the Part and Sheet Metal environments. Although not currently available for the Assembly environment, you can edit parts in the context of the top-level assembly and gain access to the annotation tools.

Practice 1a

Introduction to the Annotation Interface

Practice Objectives

- Review 3D annotations and become familiar with the annotation tools available in Autodesk Inventor part files.
- Select and edit 3D annotations.
- Relocate 3D annotations in an isometric view.
- Create a Leader Text annotation with parametric data.

In this practice, you will learn how to navigate to the annotation tools, access context menus, and how to select and review existing 3D annotations. To complete the exercise, you will edit an existing dimensional annotation and create a simple Leader Text Annotation. The completed part is shown in Figure 1–12.

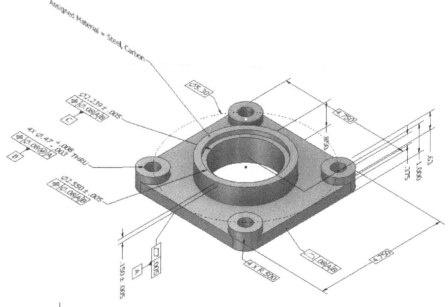

Figure 1–12

Task 1 - Open an existing part file.

1. In the *Get Started* tab>Launch panel, click (Projects) to open the Projects dialog box.

This project file is used for the entire learning guide.

2. Click **Browse**, navigate to *C:\Autodesk Inventor 2018 3D Annotations Practice Files* folder and select **Annotations.ipj**. Click **Open**. This project becomes the active one. Click **Done**.

3. Open **Flange_Bearing_Intro.ipt**. The model displays with 3D annotations already added, as shown in Figure 1–13.

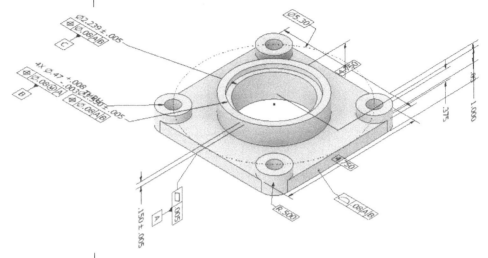

Figure 1–13

Task 2 - Review the active standard.

In this task, you will review the current Active Standard to ensure that it is set to **ASME**.

1. In the *Tools* tab>Options panel, click 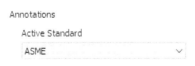 (Document Settings). In the Document Settings dialog box, select the *Standard* tab and note that the Active Standard is set as **ASME**, as shown in Figure 1–14. This was preset because the 2018 standard Imperial part template was used to create the model.

The default setting for a model created with the 2018 Metric part standard template is ***ASME - mm***.

Annotations

Active Standard

| ASME | ⌄ |

Figure 1–14

2. Close the Document Settings dialog box without making a change to the Active Standard.

Task 3 - Review the annotation interface.

In this task, you will review the tools on the *Annotate* tab, review the automatic annotation scale value, and become familiar with locating annotations in the Model Browser.

1. Select the *Annotate* tab. The options in this tab are subdivided into panels to help you find commands associated with creating GD&T annotations (Geometric Annotation panel), as well as dimensional, hole/thread notes, and surface textures (General Annotation panel). Additional text-based annotations can be created using the Notes panel.

The scale value cannot be changed in the Master Design View. Design Views are discussed in Chapter 4.

2. In the Manage panel, note that the annotation scale is set to an automatic value, as shown in Figure 1–15. This value is preset based on the current model size.

Figure 1–15

3. Use standard orientation commands (ViewCube, Pan, Zoom) to manipulate the orientation and the zoom level of the model. The annotations move with the model and the annotation scale remains unchanged.

4. Return the model to its default Home View using the ViewCube.

5. In the Model Browser, expand the **Annotations** and **Tolerance Features** folders, as shown in Figure 1–16.

   • All dimensional, hole/thread note, and surface texture annotations created in the model are listed in the **Annotations** folder. In this case, seven linear, and a single radial and diameter dimension annotation exist in the model.

   • All GD&T annotations are added to the **Tolerance Features** folder. Currently, there are five in the model.

Figure 1–16

6. Hover the cursor over the dimensional entries in the Model Browser to highlight them in the model.

7. In the **Tolerance Features** folder, hover the cursor over the **Planar Surface 1** node. This was the first GD&T annotation added to a planar surface in the model. Note that the surface selected as the planar reference for this GD&T highlights in the model.

8. Expand **Planar Surface 1**. Hover the cursor over the **Feature Control Frame 1** and the **Datum Identifier 1 (A)** entries. These highlight on the model to identify them.

Task 4 - Review the selection priority options for working with 3D annotations.

3D annotations can be selected directly in the graphics window or they can be selected in the appropriate folder in the Model Browser. When selected in one location, the annotation also highlights in the other to help identify it. In this task, you will select annotations and review the selection priority option, which enables you to easily select multiple annotations.

1. In the Quick Access Toolbar, ensure that ⬚ (Select Face and Edges) is active as the selection priority. This is generally the default selection priority that is active. This setting also enables you to select 3D annotations.

2. Select any annotation in either of the folders in the Model Browser. Once selected, the annotation is highlighted in the graphics window.

3. To select multiple annotations, press and hold <Ctrl> or <Shift> while selecting.

4. Select in the background in the graphics window to clear the selection.

5. Attempt to drag a selection window around multiple annotations in the graphics window. This cannot be done while the ⬚ (Select Face and Edges) selection priority is set.

*The **Select Annotations** selection priority can also be set using a context menu in the graphics window by pressing and holding <Shift> + right mouse button (RMB).*

6. In the Quick Access Toolbar, select ⬚ (Select Annotations) from the drop-down list, as shown in Figure 1–17.

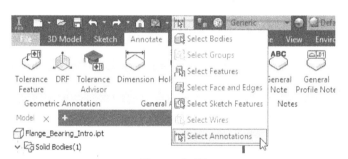

Figure 1–17

7. Return to the graphics window and drag a selection window around multiple 3D annotations. Using the **Select Annotations** selection priority, annotations are now selected.

Design Views are discussed in Chapter 4.

8. Note that with the **Select Annotations** selection priority active, you cannot select any model geometry. This option is great when manipulating the display of annotations in various Design Views, but should be left at ⬚ (Select Face and Edges) otherwise.

9. Return the selection priority to the ⬚ (Select Face and Edges) option.

Task 5 - Modify the location of annotations.

In this task, you will review the context menus and you will move and reposition existing annotations.

1. In the graphics window, select one of the **4.75** dimensional annotations and drag it into a more convenient location. Select in the background to clear the annotation's selection.

2. Move the other **4.75** dimensional annotation. Once moved, the two dimensional annotations should display similar to that shown in Figure 1–18.

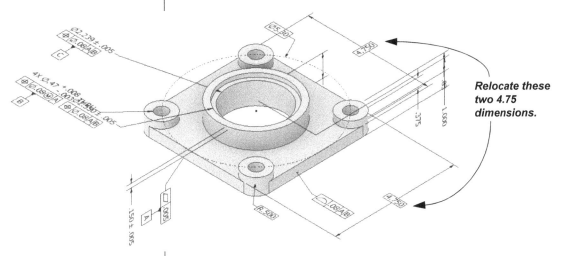

Relocate these two 4.75 dimensions.

Figure 1–18

3. In the Model Browser, select **Linear Dimension 1** and note that one of the 4.75 dimensional annotations is selected. In the Model Browser, right-click on **Linear Dimension 1** and select **Toggle Alignment**, as shown in Figure 1–19. The alignment of the dimension value flips.

Figure 1–19

4. Right-click on the other **4.75** dimensional annotation directly in the graphics window. Note that the same context menu options are available. Select **Toggle Alignment** for this annotation. The two dimensional annotations should display similar to that shown in Figure 1–20.

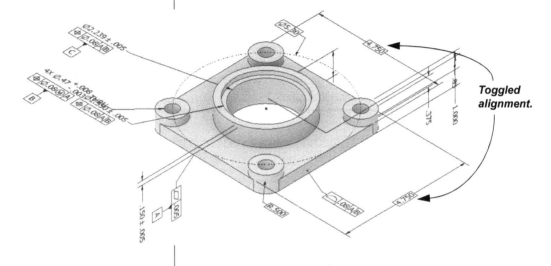

Toggled alignment.

Figure 1–20

5. Modify the locations of the remaining annotations in the model such that they display similar to that shown in Figure 1–21. To relocate annotations, select them and drag the green dots that display.

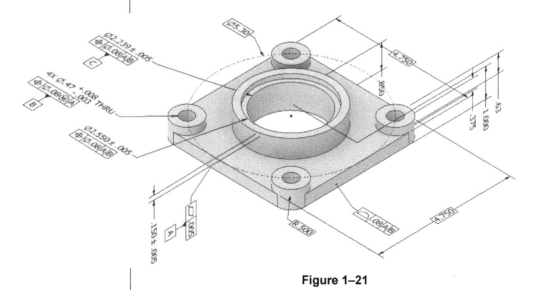

Figure 1–21

Task 6 - Modify and create an annotation.

In this task, you will learn how to make changes using the **Edit** command and how to create an annotation. This task briefly explains the creation and editing interfaces. These topics will be discussed in more depth later chapters.

1. Edit the **R.500** Radial Dimension Annotation using one of the following methods. The annotation will display as shown in Figure 1–22.

    *   In the Model Browser, right-click on **Radial Dimension 1** and select **Edit**.
    *   In the graphics window, select, right-click on the **R.500** radial dimension annotation, and select **Edit**.
    *   Alternatively, double-click on the annotation in either location.

Figure 1–22

2. Place the cursor at the beginning of the *Edit Dimension Text* field, as shown in Figure 1–23.

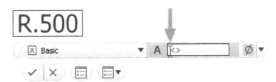

Figure 1–23

3. Enter **4 X** at the beginning of the field, as shown in Figure 1–24. Include a space before and after the X.

Figure 1–24

4. Click ✓ to complete the edit and update the annotation.

5. In the *Annotate* tab>Notes panel, click 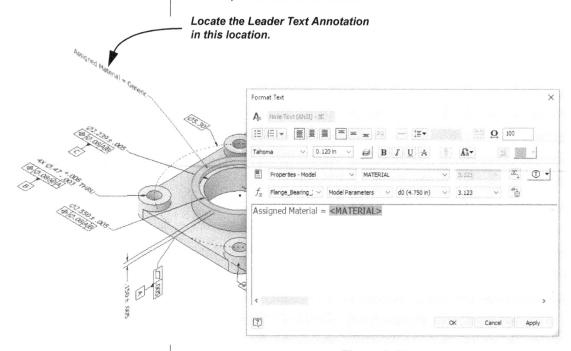 (Leader Text).

6. Select the top-most circular face on the model as the placement face and locate the annotation, as shown in Figure 1–25.

7. In the Format Text dialog box, enter the text shown in Figure 1–25. Note that the parameter *<Material>* is added by assigning the *Type* field to **Properties - Model** and the *Property* field to **MATERIAL**. Once selected, click to add the parameter to the note.

Figure 1–25

8. Click **OK** to complete the Leader Text Annotation.

9. Review the Model Browser and note that it was added to the list in the **Annotations** folder.

10. In the Quick Access Toolbar, change the material to **Steel, Carbon** and notice that the note updates to display the newly assigned material.

11. Save the model and close the window.

Chapter Review Questions

1. Which of the following statements are true regarding the process of MBD? (Select all that apply.)

    a. MBD is a process used to document a 3D model in a single 2D drawing file.

    b. MBD allows for the creation of Product Manufacturing Information (PMI) that details the requirements for manufacturing.

    c. The American Society of Mechanical Engineer standard Y14.41 (ASME Y14.41) defines the requirements for MBD.

    d. The Step format 203 supports the export of the required PMI data from a model.

2. All of the 3D annotations options available in the *Annotation* tab can also be accessed in the right-click context menu.

    a. True

    b. False

3. Which of the following are valid 3D annotations that can be created in an Autodesk Inventor part file? (Select all that apply.)

    a. Hole/Thread Notes

    b. Chamfer Notes

    c. Surface Textures

    d. Welding Symbols

4. Which of the following selection priority options enables you to select annotations in your model by dragging a selection window?

    a. **3D Annotations**

    b. **Select Features**

    c. **Select Face and Edges**

    d. **Select Annotations**

5. In which of the following locations can you set the Active Standard that defines the standard used to create 3D annotations in a model?

   a. File Menu

   b. Application Options

   c. Document Settings

   d. Projects

6. Part files created prior to Autodesk Inventor 2018 are automatically assigned an Active Standard.

   a. True

   b. False

Command Summary

Button	Command	Location
	Document Settings	• **Ribbon:** *Tools* tab>Options panel
N/A	**Select Annotations**	• **Quick Access Toolbar:** Selection Priority drop-down list • **Context Menu:** pressing and holding the <Shift> key with the RMB in Graphics Window

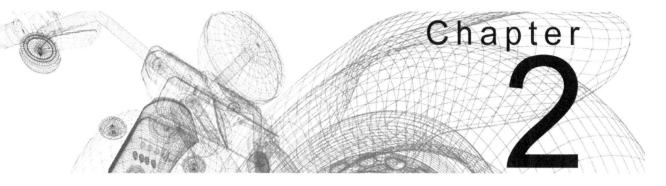

Chapter 2

3D Annotations

3D annotations can be added to a model to help communicate model information. These annotations are viewable when the model is shared as a 3D PDF or the metadata can be exported to support an MBD workflow. In either use, 3D annotations can replace the need for 2D drawing creation. In this chapter, you learn how to create 3D dimensional, hole/thread, surface texture, and informational text-based annotations.

Learning Objectives in this Chapter

- Describe which 3D annotation types can be created using the tools available in the Autodesk® Inventor® software.
- Add dimensional annotations to a model using either the promote or create methods.
- Add hole/thread note annotations to a model.
- Add surface texture annotations to a model.
- Add text-based annotations to a model to communicate additional modeling information.
- Edit existing 3D annotations in a model.

2.1 Introduction

3D annotations can reference model geometry, model dimensions and parameters, or they can simply be text-based information. 3D annotations enable you to visually describe the following:

- The size/dimensions of model geometry along with any required tolerance values. (This chapter discusses dimensional annotations; GD&T is covered in *Chapter 3*.)

- Information on holes and, if required, details on any included threads.

- Details on a specific surface finish that is required on the model once manufactured.

- Modeling notes that describe a specific feature/geometry or general notes for the model. The note can be text-based or it can include modeling parameters defined during model creation.

Figure 2–1 shows the 3D annotation tools discussed in this chapter, as well as some examples displayed on the model.

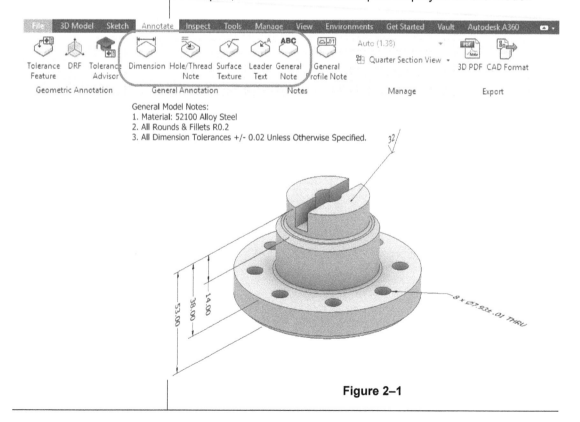

Figure 2–1

2.2 Dimensional Annotations

The inclusion of 3D dimensional annotations in a model enable you to display and visually identify the exact size, location, and acceptable tolerance values for a selected geometry.

Dimensional annotations can be created by:

- Promoting existing model dimensions.

- Creating dimensions referencing existing geometry.

Promoting vs. Creating Dimensional Annotations

Dimensional annotations display the same regardless of the placement method. Consider the following when deciding whether to promote or create dimensional annotations:

- Only visible sketch and feature dimensions can be promoted. Any other model dimension not created in a sketch or generated through feature creation, must be explicitly created as a 3D dimensional annotation.

- Promoted dimensions are easily displayed since they have already been created during the definition of the feature. Additionally, you are not required to select placement references to locate the annotation.

- Promoted dimensions are oriented as they were created and might involve less reorientation.

- Promoted dimensions include any tolerance data that was assigned when the feature was created so it does not have to be recreated.

- The feature geometry that was used to create the model might not accurately describe how the model will be manufactured and therefore the required dimensions might not explicitly exist. In these cases, you must create a new dimensional annotation.

Promoting Dimensional Annotations

Modeling dimensions can only be promoted to 3D dimensional annotations in the Model environment (not Sketch environment). Additionally, they must be sketch or feature dimensions and they must be set as visible in the model by showing the dimensions (**Show Dimensions**) for a feature or enabling sketch visibility for a sketch. To promote a visible dimension, select the value, right-click, and select **Promote**. Once promoted, you can relocate the 3D dimension annotation and clear the visibility of the sketch/feature dimension. Figure 2–2 shows this process for two different dimensions. The linear dimension shows that a tolerance value was assigned in the sketch, but the diameter value does not have a tolerance value assigned.

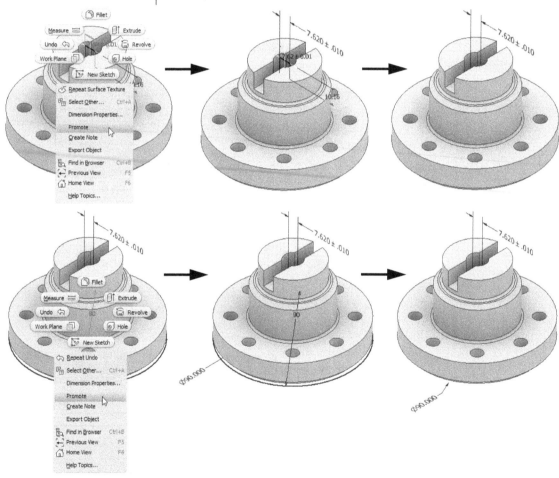

1. *Enable sketch visibility or Show Dimensions.*
2. *Select the dimension.*
3. *Right-click and select Promote.*

4. *Select the new Dimension annotation and drag/relocate it on the 3D model, as required.*

4. *Toggle off the visibility of the sketch.*

Figure 2–2

When creating the geometry for your 3D model, consider whether dimensions are required for display as 3D dimensional annotation. If so, ensure that the dimension is included in the sketch or feature creation, so that it can be promoted. If the dimension is not provided during model creation, you can create it explicitly as described in the following section.

Creating Dimensional Annotations

A 3D dimensional annotation can be created as linear, angular, and radius/diameter dimensions, as shown in Figure 2–3.

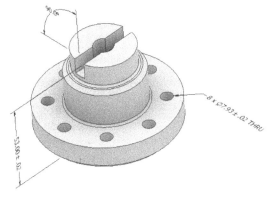

Figure 2–3

How To: Create a Dimensional Annotation.

1. In the *Annotate* tab>General Annotation panel, click

   (Dimension).

2. Select references on the model to define the dimension.
   - Select an edge to dimension its length as a linear dimension.
   - Select two vertices or a combination of vertices and edges to create a linear dimension.
   - Select two parallel edges to dimension the linear distance between them. Workplanes and/or axis can also be selected to define the distance between them.
   - Select two faces or two planes that are at an angle to one another to create an angular dimension.
   - Select a cylindrical face or edge to create a diameter/radius dimension.

3. If the dimension type does not display as required, right-click and select an alternate dimension type on the **Dimension Type** menu.

- The options for linear dimensions include **Horizontal**, **Vertical**, and **Aligned**.
- The options for diameter/radius dimensions include **Radius** and **Diameter**.

The options available for selecting an alternate annotation plane are dependent on the dimension being created.

4. Default annotation planes are generated to locate the dimension. It is based on the selected location on the reference. You can accept the provided annotation plane or select an alternate.

- Press the <Space Bar> or right-click and select **Select Next Candidate Plane** to toggle between the available default options.
- If the provided default annotation plane(s) are not appropriate, press <Shift> or right-click and select **Select Annotation Plane**. Once activated, select an existing model face or work plane.

The options available for reorienting an annotation are dependent on the dimension being created.

5. (Optional) Once the annotation plane is active, and prior to selecting a placement location for the annotation, you can access options to align the annotation to existing references.

- Right-click and select **Align to Geometry** and select an edge or work axis. This alignment is temporary and if you move the cursor, the alignment is lost. Select in the graphics window to locate the annotation without moving the mouse.
- Right-click and select **Toggle Alignment** to flip the orientation of the annotation, as shown in Figure 2–4.

The orientation of the annotation can be flipped using the Toggle Alignment option.

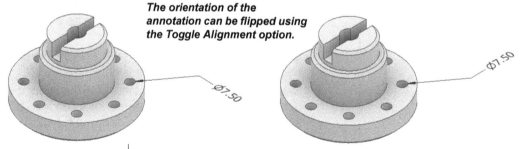

Figure 2–4

6. Select in the graphics window to locate the dimensional annotation. Once placed, the dimension is assigned and a mini-toolbar displays, similar to that for the linear dimension shown in Figure 2–5.

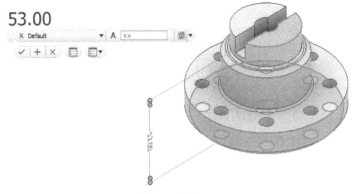

Figure 2–5

7. Define the tolerance for the dimensional annotation.

- Expand the Tolerance drop-down list and select the tolerance type, as shown in Figure 2–6.
- Select the tolerance value to open a second mini-toolbar to define its value and precision, as shown in Figure 2–7.

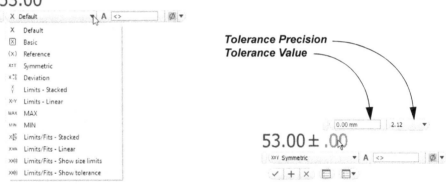

Figure 2–6   **Figure 2–7**

- Enter additional text or symbols either before or after the < > symbols, as shown in Figure 2–8.

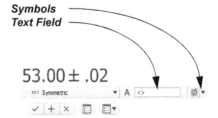

Figure 2–8

Special symbols can only be added to a dimensional annotation using the Edit Dimension dialog box.

- To set tolerances, add text, or special symbols, select ⊞ to use the Edit Dimension dialog box. This dialog box is the same as in the drawing environment.

8. Click ✓ to complete the dimensional annotation.

Editing Dimensional Annotations

Once created, dimensional annotations are displayed on the model and are listed in the **Annotations** folder in the Model Browser. To edit an existing dimension annotation:

- Right-click on the dimension annotation in the Model Browser or in the graphics window and select **Edit**. Alternatively, you can double-click on it. The same mini-toolbar used to create it displays for editing.

- Right-click on the dimension annotation in the Model Browser or in the graphics window and select any of the options shown in Figure 2–9 to make changes to the alignment, visibility, text, precision, and arrowhead display (**Options**). The options are dependent on the type of dimension being edited.

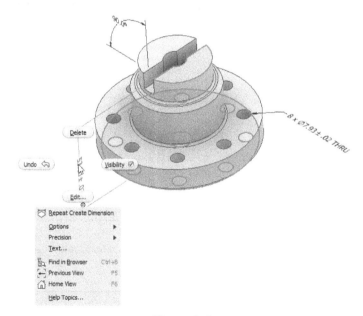

Figure 2–9

- Select an annotation to activate it. Select and drag the green circular references on the extension or leader lines to change its location on the annotation plane or relative to the measured reference.

2.3 Hole/Thread Note Annotations

Hole and thread notes can be added as 3D annotations to communicate how a hole is to be manufactured. The information that populates this type of annotation is pulled from the geometry and features used to create it. Thread information is recognized in a model whether it was added during hole creation or if it was added using the **Thread** command. The model shown in Figure 2–10 shows two different hole/thread note annotations that were created in the model.

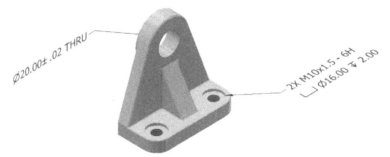

Figure 2–10

How To: Create a Hole/Thread Note Annotation.

1. In the *Annotate* tab>General Annotation panel, click

    (Hole/Thread Note).
2. Select a cylindrical face on the model geometry to choose the hole.
3. The annotation plane defines the plane on which the 3D annotation will be placed. If the default annotation plane does not display as required, consider using the following options:
   - Press <Space Bar> or right-click and select **Select Next Candidate Plane** to toggle between the default options, if available.
   - Press <Shift> or right-click and select **Select Annotation Plane** to select a specific plane. The selected plane must be perpendicular to the hole.

4. (Optional) Once the annotation plane is active, and prior to selecting a placement location for the annotation, you can access options to align the annotation to existing references.

- Right-click, select **Align to Geometry**, and then select an edge or work axis. This alignment is temporary and if you move the cursor, the alignment is lost. Select in the graphics window to locate the annotation without moving the mouse.

- Right-click and select **Toggle Alignment** to flip the orientation of the annotation, as shown in Figure 2–11.

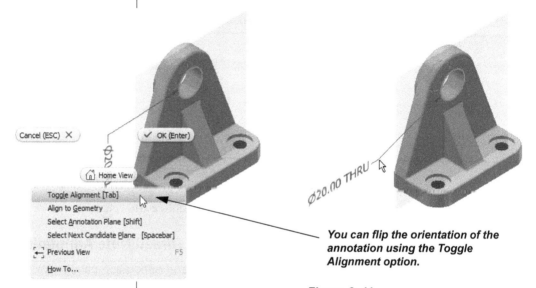

You can flip the orientation of the annotation using the Toggle Alignment option.

Figure 2–11

5. Select a location in the graphics window to place the annotation on the defined plane. The annotation mini-toolbar displays to define the annotation, as shown in Figure 2–12.

Figure 2–12

6. Use the mini-toolbar to complete the following:

- Review the hole type. This is read from the model and cannot be changed.

- Select **Use Global Precision** to use the precision from the model. If this option is disabled, you are able to modify the precision for the hole values in the annotation.

- Select **Use Part Tolerance** to use the part tolerance from the model. If this option is disabled, you are able to modify the tolerance for the hole values in the annotation.

7. Select the hole dimension value and modify its precision or tolerance (as shown in Figure 2–13), if required. The availability of these fields are dependent on whether the **Use Global Precision** and **Use Part Tolerance** options were enabled.

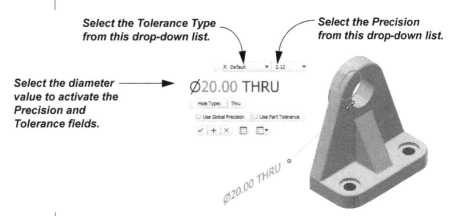

Select the Tolerance Type from this drop-down list.

Select the Precision from this drop-down list.

Select the diameter value to activate the Precision and Tolerance fields.

Figure 2–13

- The hole diameter value cannot be modified because it is based on the model geometry.

- To define the tolerance values, select the value that displays when the tolerance type is selected and enter a new value in the entry field.

8. To add special symbols in a value field, select [icon]. This dialog box is the same as that used to create hole notes in a drawing.

9. Click [icon] to complete the hole/thread note annotation.

Editing Hole/Thread Note Annotations

Once created, hole/thread note annotations display on the model and are listed in the **Annotations** folder in the Model Browser. To edit them, consider the following:

- Right-click on the hole/thread note annotation in the Model Browser or in the graphics window and select **Edit**. Alternatively, you can double-click on it. The same mini-toolbar used to create it displays for editing.

- Right-click on the hole/thread note annotation in the Model Browser or in the graphics window and select any of the options shown in Figure 2–14 to make changes to its alignment or visibility.

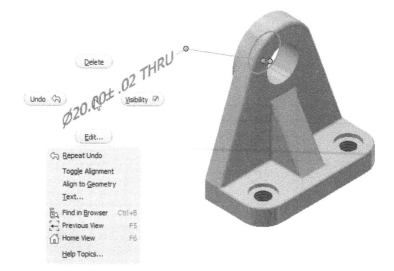

Figure 2–14

- Right-click on the hole/thread note annotation in the Model Browser or in the graphics window and select **Text**. The standard Format Text dialog box opens, as shown in Figure 2–15. This dialog box enables you to add text before or after the parametric hole/thread information.

The Format Text dialog box cannot be used to add additional parameters.

Figure 2–15

- Select an annotation in the Model Browser or in the graphics window to activate it. Select and drag the green circular reference at the elbow of the annotation (leader line/ extension line) to change the location of the annotation on the circular edge.

- Select an annotation in the Model Browser or in the graphics window to activate it. Select the annotation text and drag it to change its location on the extension line.

2.4 Surface Texture Annotations

Surface texture symbols can be added as 3D annotations to communicate special surface finishes for faces on the model. Figure 2–16 shows an example of a surface texture annotation added to a model.

If a unique surface finish is required during manufacturing, surface texture annotations are also needed. This requirement is regardless of whether you are planning to export the design as a Step 242 file format or simply view it as a 3D PDF. This is because there is no other modeling tool that enables assignment of a surface finish.

Figure 2–16

How To: Create a Surface Texture Annotation.

1. In the *Annotate* tab>General Annotation panel, click

    (Surface Texture).
2. Select the face on the model that requires a unique surface finish.
3. The annotation plane defines the plane on which the annotation will be placed. If the default annotation plane does not display as required, consider using the following options:

   - Press <Space Bar> or right-click and select **Select Next Candidate Plane** to toggle between the default options, if available (as shown in Figure 2–17).

The selected location on the face defines where the leader points.

The surface texture annotation is added to this face (highlights in blue).

Default annotation plane is located perpendicular and through the selected point on the annotation face.

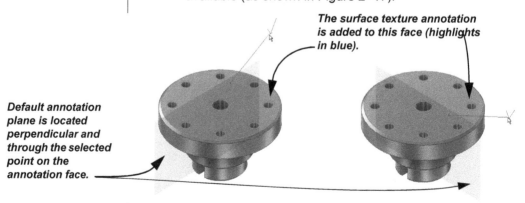

Figure 2–17

- Press <Shift> or right-click and select **Select Annotation Plane** to select a specific plane. The selected plane must be perpendicular to the face.

4. (Optional) Once the annotation plane is active, and prior to selecting a placement location for the annotation, you can access options to align the annotation to existing references.

   - Right-click, select **Align to Geometry**, and then select an edge or work axis. This alignment is temporary and if you move the cursor, the alignment is lost. Select to locate the annotation without moving the mouse.

   - Right-click and select **Toggle Alignment** to flip the orientation of the annotation, as shown in Figure 2–18.

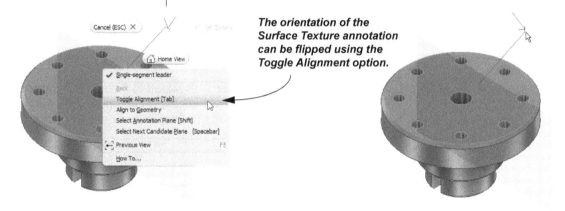

The orientation of the Surface Texture annotation can be flipped using the Toggle Alignment option.

Figure 2–18

5. Select a location in the graphics window to place the annotation on the defined plane. The annotation mini-toolbar displays to define the annotation, as shown in Figure 2–19.

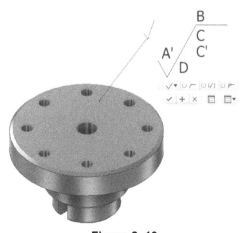

Figure 2–19

6. Use the mini-toolbar to define the options for the surface texture annotation.

   • Select the required surface texture symbol from the list, as shown in Figure 2–20.

   • Select the **Force Tail**, **Majority**, or **All-around** options (as shown in Figure 2–21), as required, to modify the symbol.

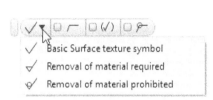

Figure 2–20

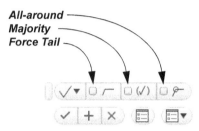

Figure 2–21

   • Select any of the letters displayed in the symbol preview to activate its value field, as shown in Figure 2–22 for A (roughness average max). Enter the necessary finish values for the required fields.

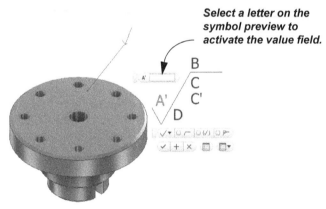

Figure 2–22

   • To add special symbols in a value field, you must select ⊟ to activate the same dialog box used to create surface texture symbols in a drawing. This dialog box provides access to additional symbols.

7. Click ✓ to complete the surface texture annotation.

Editing Surface Texture Annotations

Once created, surface texture annotations are displayed on the model and are listed in the **Annotations** folder in the Model Browser. To edit an existing surface texture annotation, consider the following:

- Right-click on the surface texture annotation in the Model Browser or in the graphics window and select **Edit**. Alternatively, you can double-click on it. The same mini-toolbar used to create it displays for editing.

- Right-click on the surface texture annotation in the Model Browser or in the graphics window and select any of the options shown in Figure 2–23 to make changes to its alignment, visibility, or to add a vertex to the annotation's leader.

Figure 2–23

- Select an annotation in the Model Browser or in the graphics window to activate it. Select and drag any of the green circular references to change the location of the annotation on the face or on the extension line.

- Select an annotation in the Model Browser or in the graphics window to activate it. Select the annotation to change its location on the annotation plane.

2.5 Text-Based Annotations

The **Leader Text** and **General Note** options can be used to communicate additional text-based model information in the form of a 3D annotation. Leader text annotations reference model geometry and use annotation planes for placement. General note annotations are added to one of the four screen quadrants and do not reorient when the model is rotated. Figure 2–24 shows an example of a general note shown in the top-left quadrant (quadrant 2) and a leader text annotation.

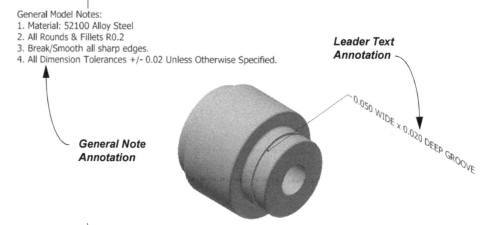

General Model Notes:
1. Material: 52100 Alloy Steel
2. All Rounds & Fillets R0.2
3. Break/Smooth all sharp edges.
4. All Dimension Tolerances +/- 0.02 Unless Otherwise Specified.

Leader Text Annotation

0.050 WIDE X 0.020 DEEP GROOVE

General Note Annotation

Figure 2–24

How To: Create Leader Text Annotations.

1. In the *Annotate* tab>Notes panel, click ⬜ (Leader Text).
2. Select a vertex, edge, or face to set the anchor point for the leader. For edges and faces, select the exact location on the entity to define the anchor point.
3. Select the annotation plane. This defines the plane on which the leader text annotation is placed. If the default annotation plane does not display as required, consider using the following options:
   - Press <Space Bar> or right-click and select **Select Next Candidate Plane** to toggle between the default options, if available. Figure 2–25 shows three default annotation planes that are available for use based on the selection of the cylindrical face (undercut).

Figure 2–25

- Press <Shift> or right-click and select **Select Annotation Plane** to select a specific plane. Once activated, select an existing model face or work plane. The annotation plane is still created through the point that was selected, but its placement remains parallel with the new reference.

4. (Optional) Once the annotation plane is active, and prior to selecting a placement location for the annotation, you can access options to align the annotation to existing references.

   - Right-click, select **Align to Geometry**, and select an edge or work axis. This alignment is temporary and if you move the cursor, the alignment is lost. Select to locate the annotation without moving the mouse.
   - Right-click and select **Toggle Alignment** to flip the orientation of the annotation.

5. Select a location in the graphics window to place the annotation on the defined annotation plane. The standard Format Text dialog box displays to define the text for the annotation, as shown in Figure 2–26.

Without text to define the annotation, its orientation is difficult to identify. These options can also be accessed during the editing stage.

The values for assigned parameters display in gray highlight.

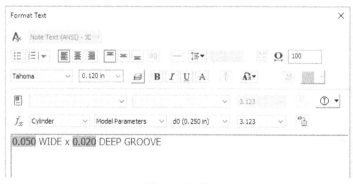

Figure 2–26

The font size set in the Format Text dialog box can be additionally scaled if the Design View's annotation scale is changed.

6. Use the Format Text dialog box to enter text and assign model parameters to define the annotation.
7. Click **OK** in the Format Text dialog box to complete the leader text annotation.

Multi-Segment Leaders

By default, the leader text annotation is created with a single-segment leader. To create it with multiple segments, prior to placing the annotation, right-click and clear the **Single-Segment Leader** option in the context menu. Once cleared, it remains cleared until the option is selected again.

How To: Create General Note Annotations.

1. In the *Annotate* tab>Notes panel, click ⬡ ABC (General Note).
2. Select one of the four quadrants around the graphics window to place the annotation.
3. Use the Format Text dialog box to enter text and assign model parameters, as required. As text is entered, a preview displays in the graphics window.
4. Click **OK** in the Format Text dialog box to complete the general note annotation.

The annotation scale in a Design View does not control the size of the text. It must be set in the Format Text dialog box.

Editing Text-Based Annotations

Once created, text-based annotations created using either the **Leader Text** or **General Note** options display on the model and are listed in the **Annotations** folder in the Model Browser. To edit either of these annotations, consider the following:

- Right-click on a name in the Model Browser and select **Edit**. Alternatively, you can double-click on it. The Format Text dialog box used to create them displays for editing.

- Right-click on any leader text annotation in the graphics window and select **Edit**. The Format Text dialog box used to create it displays for editing. General note annotations cannot be accessed directly in the graphics window unless the **Select Annotations** selection priority is active.

The location of General Notes cannot be modified once they are placed. You will have to recreate it to place it in another quadrant.

- For leader text annotations, select it in the Model Browser or in the graphics window to activate it. Select and drag any of the green circular references to change the location of the annotation on the face or on the extension line. Alternatively, select and drag it to change location on the annotation plane.

Practice 2a | Adding 3D Annotations

Practice Objectives

- Promote and create 3D dimensional annotations.
- Create hole/thread note annotations.
- Create surface texture annotations.
- Create text-based annotations using leader and general notes.
- Edit 3D annotations in a model.

In this practice, you will create the 3D annotations shown in Figure 2–27. They are all created using the options available in the General Annotation and Notes panels in the *Annotate* tab. As you progress through the practice, you will learn how to create the annotations and make edits to them. In the final task, you will simply be provided with an image and asked to create the remaining annotations to practice your new skills.

General Notes:
1. All Dimension Tolerances +/- 0.1 Unless Otherwise Specified.
2. Material: Cast Bronze with surface finishes as noted.

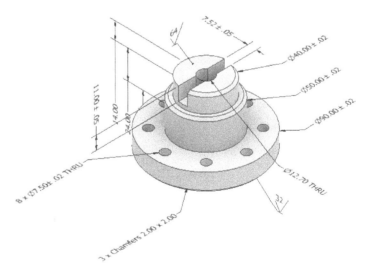

Figure 2–27

Task 1 - Review the active standard.

In this task, you will review the current Active Standard to ensure that it is set to **ASME - mm**.

1. Open **Locking Hub.ipt**.

2. In the *Tools* tab>Options panel, click  (Document Settings). In the Document Settings dialog box, select the *Standard* tab and note that the Active Standard (shown in Figure 2–28) is set to **ASME - mm**. This was preset because the 2018 standard Metric part template was used to create the model.

*The default setting for a model created with the 2018 Imperial part standard template is **ASME**.*

Annotations

Active Standard

| ASME - mm | ⌄ |

Figure 2–28

3. Close the Document Settings dialog box without making a change to the Active Standard.

Task 2 - Promote model dimensions to dimensional annotations.

In this task, you will learn to promote existing sketch dimensions.

1. Toggle on the visibility of **Sketch1**. This is the sketch associated with the **Revolution1** feature.

2. Select the **Bottom** view on the ViewCube so that it is easy to recognize the dimension values.

3. Right-click on the **15** dimension value and select **Promote**, as shown in Figure 2–29. If prompted to specify the annotation standard, confirm that it is set to **ASME - mm** and click **OK**.

*Alternatively, you can select the **Revolution1** feature, right-click, and select **Show Dimensions** to also access the **Promote** option.*

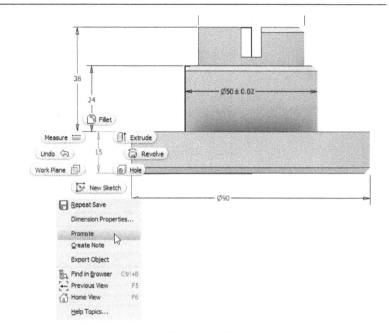

Figure 2–29

4. Return the model to its default Home View. The dimension annotation should display similar to that shown in Figure 2–30, in both the graphics window and the Model Browser. The sketch dimensions are still being shown so they temporarily overlap while the sketch is visible.

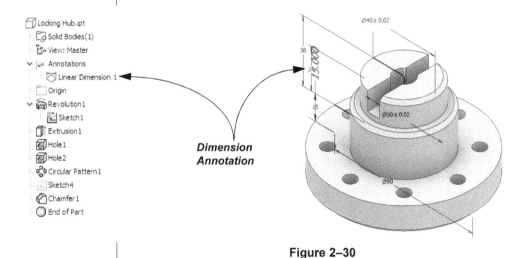

Figure 2–30

5. Promote the following dimensions from the displayed sketch. The annotations should display as shown in Figure 2–31.

- **24** linear dimension
- **Ø40 +/- 0.020** diameter dimension
- **Ø50 +/- 0.020** diameter dimension
- **Ø90** diameter dimension

*It may be easier to view and select the dimensions from the **Bottom** view.*

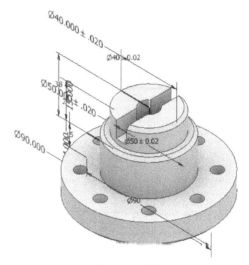

Figure 2–31

6. Review the new dimensional annotations and note the following:

- The **Ø40** and **Ø50** diameter dimensions had tolerance values assigned in the sketch. Once promoted, these values are included. The **Ø90** diameter dimension does not have the tolerance set in the sketch so this has to be added manually.
- The remaining linear dimension (38mm) is not the required value required for the annotation. The dimensioning scheme for the sketch does not include the final linear dimension required. This dimensional annotation has to be explicitly created.

7. Toggle off the visibility of the sketch.

Task 3 - Create a linear dimension annotation.

In this task, you will learn how to create dimensional annotations.

1. Toggle on the visibility of the **XZ Plane** in the **Origin** folder. This plane will be used as the annotation plane for a new annotation so that it remains planar with the other annotations that were previously promoted.

2. In the *Annotate* tab>General Annotation panel, click

    (Dimension).

3. Select the two faces shown in Figure 2–32 as the references for the new annotation.

Note that the other dimensional annotations have been cleared from the display for clarity.

Select these two planar references to define the new linear dimension annotation.

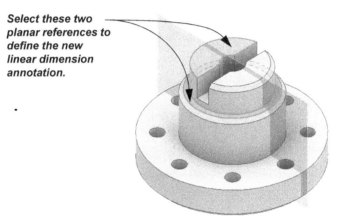

Figure 2–32

4. Once the second reference is selected, a 14.00 linear dimension displays on the screen and moves with the cursor. This dimension may not display on the same plane as the other linear dimension annotations. Right-click and select **Select Annotation Plane**. Select the displayed XZ Plane to change its placement plane.

*If the assumed dimension type is not as required, right-click and select an alternate dimension type on the **Dimension Type** menu.*

5. Select in the graphics window to locate the dimension annotation. Once placed, the dimension is assigned and a mini-toolbar displays as shown in Figure 2–33.

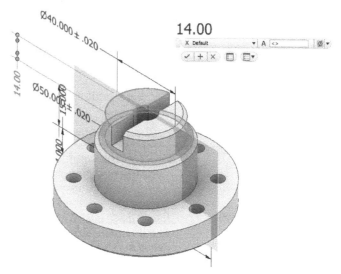

Figure 2–33

6. Click 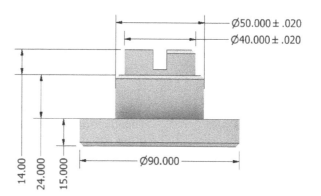 to complete the dimension annotation. The tolerance value will be modified later in this exercise.

7. Reorient the model to the **Bottom** view and select and drag the annotations similar to that shown in Figure 2–34.

Click and hold an annotation to move the text.

Figure 2–34

Task 4 - Create a diameter dimension annotation.

In this task, you will learn how to create a diameter dimensional annotation and assign a tolerance value.

1. Return the model to its Default Home View and toggle off the display of the XZ Plane.

2. In the Model Browser, expand the new **Annotations** folder. This folder contains all the dimensional annotations that have just been created (promoted and created). Hover the cursor over each annotation in the list to review them on the model.

3. The three diameter dimensions display as linear because they were linear in the sketch. Select the **Ø40.000** dimensional annotation, right-click, and select **Delete**.

4. Delete the **Ø50.000** and **Ø90.000** dimensional annotations.

5. In the *Annotate* tab>General Annotation panel, click

   (Dimension).

6. Select the cylindrical face of the smallest cylinder. A radius value displays. Prior to placing the dimension, right-click and select **Dimension Type>Diameter**.

7. Click to place the dimension annotation on the default annotation plane.

8. Expand the mini-toolbar and select **Symmetric**, as shown in Figure 2–35 to set the tolerance type.

Figure 2–35

9. Select the symmetric **.00** tolerance value at the top of the mini-toolbar.

10. Enter **0.02mm** in the mini-toolbar that displays as shown in Figure 2–36.

Figure 2–36

11. Click 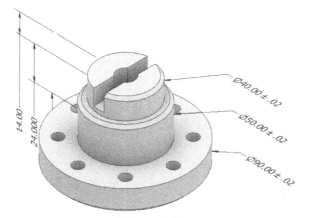 to complete the dimensional annotation. The process of creating the dimension, setting the Tolerance type, and setting its tolerance value is consistent for all dimension types.

12. Create the **Ø50.000** and **Ø90.000** dimensional annotations (including tolerance values), as shown in Figure 2–37.

Figure 2–37

Task 5 - Modify dimensional annotations.

In this task, you will learn how to change dimension precision and modify the orientation of an annotation.

1. Right-click on the **24.000** linear dimension and select **Precision>2.12 - [1/4]**, as shown in Figure 2–38. This step updates the precision to match that of the 14.00 created dimension.

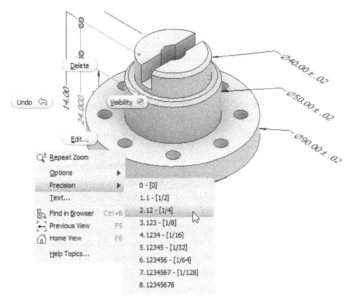

Figure 2–38

2. Change the precision for the **15.000** linear dimension annotation as described in the previous step.

3. Right-click on the **Ø90.00** dimension annotation and select **Toggle Alignment** to flip its orientation. Additionally, toggle the alignment of the **Ø40.00** and **Ø50.00** annotations. The model displays similar to that shown in Figure 2–39.

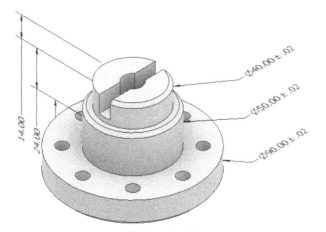

Figure 2–39

4. Right-click on the **24.00** linear dimension annotation. Note that you cannot toggle the alignment for linear dimension annotations. The inability to toggle also occurs when creating a linear dimension annotation.

Task 6 - Create a surface texture annotation.

In this task, you will learn how to create a simple surface texture annotation.

1. In the *Annotate* tab>General Annotation panel, click

    (Surface Texture).

2. Select the face shown in Figure 2–40 to place the surface texture annotation. The selected face describes the face that will have the unique surface texture finish applied.

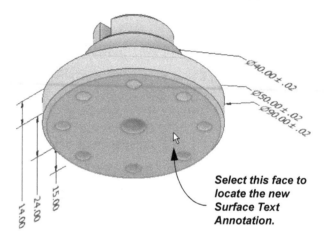

Select this face to locate the new Surface Text Annotation.

Figure 2–40

3. The default annotation plane is generated perpendicular to the selected face and through the selected point.

4. Return the model to its default Home View using the ViewCube. Surface texture annotation creation remain active. The default placement plane may not display as required. Press <Space Bar> or right-click and select **Next Candidate Plane** to toggle between the two default options. Once the annotation plane displays as shown in Figure 2–41, select to place the surface texture annotation.

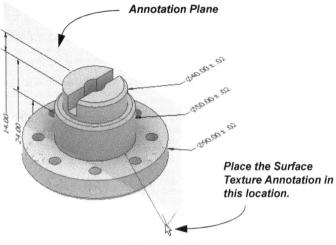

Figure 2–41

5. Once the annotation is placed, a mini-toolbar displays to define the surface texture annotation. Expand the Surface Texture Type drop-down list, as shown in Figure 2–42. This pull-down list includes the types of symbols available. Leave the default option (**Basic Surface texture symbol**) selected.

6. Select the A' symbol in the annotation. This value is the roughness average max value. Enter **32** in the entry field, as shown in Figure 2–43.

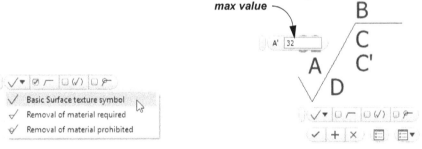

Figure 2–42   **Figure 2–43**

7. Although no additional options are required to define the surface texture annotation, you can further customize the values, and define the symbol that displays by selecting the **Force Tail**, **Majority**, or **All-around** options, as required.

8. Without making any further changes to the surface texture annotation, click ✓ to complete it.

Task 7 - Create a hole/thread note annotation.

In this task, you will learn how to create a hole/thread note annotation.

1. In the *Annotate* tab>General Annotation panel, click
     (Hole/Thread Note).

2. Select the cylindrical hole face shown in Figure 2–44 to define the hole for the annotation.

3. When selecting a face, the default annotation plane may not display as required. In this case, the annotation plane should be the planar face on which the holes are located. Rotating the model prior to placement helps you determine if the plane displays as required. If it does not, press <Shift> or right-click and select **Select Annotation Plane**, and select the face shown in Figure 2–44.

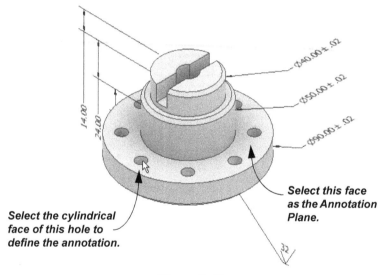

Figure 2–44

4. Once the annotation plane is active, and prior to selecting its placement location, right-click and select **Toggle Alignment** to flip the orientation of the annotation, as shown in Figure 2–45.

Toggle the alignment so the annotation displays like this.

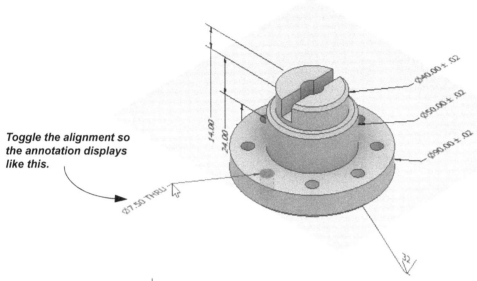

Figure 2–45

Tolerances for hole/thread note annotations are set the same way as dimension tolerances. Refer to Task 5 to review this process, if required.

5. The annotation mini-toolbar displays to define the annotation. The annotation recognizes that the feature is a thru hole. Using the mini-toolbar, set the *Tolerance Type* to **Symmetric** and set the value to **0.02**.

6. Click ✓ to complete the hole/thread note annotation.

7. Right-click on the hole/thread note annotation and select **Text**.

When editing the text for hole/thread note annotations, you cannot incorporate the use of parameters in the annotation.

8. Edit the text to show that there are 8 holes, as shown in Figure 2–46.

Figure 2–46

9. Click **OK** to complete the annotation. It should display similar to that shown in Figure 2–47.

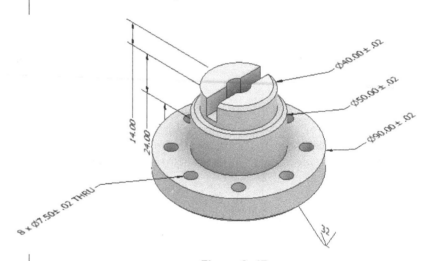

Figure 2–47

Task 8 - Add annotation notes to the model.

In this task, you will learn how to create a leader text and general note annotations.

1. In the *Annotate* tab>Notes panel, click **ABC** (General Note).

2. Select top-left quadrant (quadrant 2) in the graphics window to place the annotation. The Format Text dialog box opens.

The annotation scale does not control the size of the text. It is set in the Format Text dialog box.

3. Enter the text as shown in Figure 2–48 to define the text for the general note annotation. As you enter the text, a preview displays on the model.

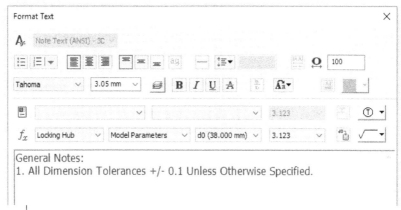

Figure 2–48

4. Click **OK** in the Format Text dialog box. The model displays similar to that shown in Figure 2–49.

General Notes:
1. All Dimension Tolerances +/- 0.1 Unless Otherwise Specified.

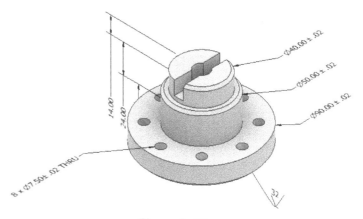

Figure 2–49

*If the **Select Annotations** filter is enabled, you can also right-click on it and select **Edit** or double-click to edit it.*

5. To make changes to a general note annotation, you must access it in the Model Browser. You are only able to edit the text or delete it. To reposition in another quadrant you must delete and recreate.

6. Open the Parameters dialog box. Scroll through the list and note that **d33** is consumed by **Chamfer1**. This dimension is 2mm and it is the value that defines the chamfer. This parameter name will be used in an upcoming step. Close the Parameters dialog box.

7. In the *Annotate* tab>Notes panel, click 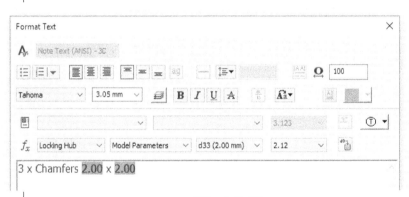 (Leader Text).

8. Select the edge at the bottom of the largest cylinders. This is where one of three chamfers is located.

9. Accept the default annotation plane and place the annotation. The standard Format Text dialog box displays.

The font size set in the Format Text dialog box can be used to individually scale the annotation regardless of the Design View's annotation scale.

10. Enter the text as shown in Figure 2–50.

- Enter the non-highlighted text using the keyboard.
- The values for assigned parameters display in gray highlight. To assign parameters, find them in the Model Parameters List (**d33**), set the precision (**2.12**), and add them using .

Figure 2–50

11. Click **OK** in the Format Text dialog box to complete the leader text annotation. The model should display similar to that shown in Figure 2–51. Chamfer notes cannot be explicitly created. Consider using leader text and parameters to capture the chamfer data as a 3D annotation.

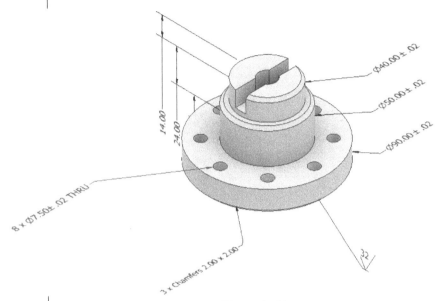

Figure 2–51

12. Save the model.

Summary

In this exercise, you learned to create five different 3D annotation types (**Dimension**, **Hole/Thread Note**, **Surface Texture**, **General Note**, and **Leader Text**). Generally, the process for creating each are very similar. The tasks showed you the available options in at least one of the annotation types. Continue to use the context menus as you locate annotations to be aware of your options. In this exercise, the **Align to Geometry** option was not used as it is not commonly required in a cylindrical model.

Task 9 - (Optional) Add additional 3D annotations to the model.

- Continue practicing creating the additional annotations shown in Figure 2–52. Note that the general note annotation has been edited to add a new line item. A completed model **Locking Hub Final.ipt** is provided in the practice files folder for review, if required.

General Notes:
1. All Dimension Tolerances +/- 0.1 Unless Otherwise Specified.
2. Material: Cast Bronze with surface finishes as noted.

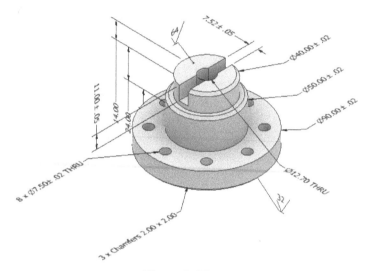

Figure 2–52

Chapter Review Questions

1. When a dimensional annotation is added using the **Promote** option, you must explicitly assign the tolerance value even if it was assigned to the model dimension during feature creation.

   a. True

   b. False

2. Which of the following context menu options are available for defining the annotation plane that will be used to place a newly created dimension annotation? (Select all that apply.)

   a. **Select Next Candidate Plane**

   b. **Select Annotation Plane**

   c. **Align to Geometry**

   d. **Toggle Alignment**

3. Which of the following options on the mini-toolbar (shown in Figure 2–53) enable you to include text as a portion of the dimension annotation. (Select all that apply.)

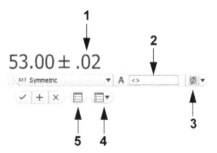

Figure 2–53

   a. 1

   b. 2

   c. 3

   d. 4

   e. 5

4. Thread information is only recognized in a model if it was added during hole creation. Thread information added using the Thread option is not automatically recognized.

   a. True

   b. False

5. The precision of the hole diameter assigned in a hole/thread note annotation can only be controlled by the part model.

   a. True

   b. False

6. Which of the following reference types must be selected to define a surface texture annotation?

   a. Face/Surface

   b. Edge

   c. Point

   d. Work Plane

7. Which of the following options on the mini-toolbar (shown in Figure 2–54) enable you to change the type of surface texture symbol (i.e., Removal of material required).

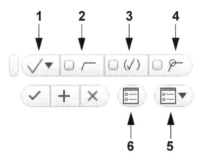

Figure 2–54

   a. 1

   b. 2

   c. 3

   d. 4

   e. 5

   f. 6

8. Which of the following 3D annotation types cannot be relocated once it has been placed?

    a. Dimension

    b. Hole/Thread Note

    c. Surface Texture

    d. Leader Text

    e. General Note

9. To which of the following 3D annotation types can you assign a parameter? (Select all that apply.)

    a. Dimension

    b. Hole/Thread Note

    c. Surface Texture

    d. Leader Text

    e. General Note

10. When placing a general note annotation, you must select an annotation plane to locate it.

    a. True

    b. False

Command Summary

Button	Command	Location
	Dimension	• **Ribbon:** *Annotate* tab>General Annotation panel
	General Note	• **Ribbon:** *Annotate* tab>Notes panel
	Hole/Thread Note	• **Ribbon:** *Annotate* tab>General Annotation panel
	Leader Text	• **Ribbon:** *Annotate* tab>Notes panel
NA	Promote	• **Context Menu:** in graphics window with a sketch or feature dimension selected
	Surface Texture	• **Ribbon:** *Annotate* tab>General Annotation panel

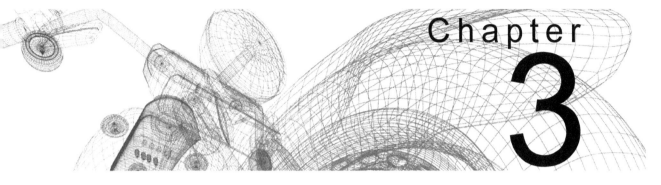

Geometric Annotations

In the previous chapter, the 3D annotations discussed focused on dimensional data, hole/thread information, surface finish instructions, and general notes. This chapter will focus on adding geometric tolerance information as tolerance features or geometry profile note annotations.

Learning Objectives in this Chapter

- Add tolerance features to a model.
- Create datum reference frames.
- Use the Tolerance Advisor to review informational messages and warnings on the tolerance features in a model.
- Create general profile note annotation.

Knowledge of GD&T required.

The international GD&T standard, ASME Y14.5M-1994, governs how annotations should be added to clearly describe the model's intent. This section of the learning guide assumes that you know how the model is to be annotated and only aims to explain how to use the **Tolerance Feature** command.

3.1 Introduction

The geometry designed in a 3D CAD modeling environment can be created perfectly. During the manufacturing stage, it is not possible to achieve the same perfection. Variations in size, feature location, and orientation are unavoidable. Using the 3D annotation types discussed in *Chapter 2*, you learned how to communicate some dimensional tolerance data to improve manufacturing accuracy, but the inclusion of geometric dimensioning and tolerancing (GD&T) annotations takes it one step further by including geometric tolerance types. GD&T standards are internationally accepted and use a symbol-based system for tolerance control. Geometric symbols are used to define tolerance zones as well as the relationships between geometry to accurately define the model's design intent. Figure 3–1 shows an example of a model that contains GD&T annotations.

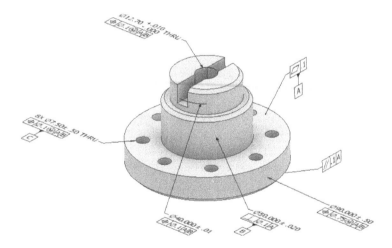

Figure 3–1

With GD&T, the assigned symbols and values define the specifications for the part to function according to the design intent. Assigning GD&T annotations that set a tighter allowance than required can make parts harder to manufacture and comes at a much higher manufacturing cost. A balance between fit and function is key.

This chapter focuses on the GD&T annotations that can be added in an Autodesk Inventor model using the **Tolerance Feature** command.

3.2 Tolerance Features

The **Tolerance Feature** command enables you to attach GD&T annotations to faces of a 3D model to accurately define the acceptable size variations during manufacturing.

> **Knowledge of GD&T required.**
>
> The international GD&T standard, ASME Y14.5M-1994, governs how annotations should be added to clearly describe the model's intent. This section of the learning guide assumes that you know how the model is to be annotated and only aims to explain how to use the **Tolerance Feature** command.

How To: Create a Tolerance Feature.

1. In the *Annotate* tab>Geometric Annotation panel, click

    (Tolerance Feature).

2. Select a face on the model geometry to define its GD&T annotation. The selected location on the face defines where the feature control frame is connected.

   - The mini-toolbar that displays during face selection provides you with options to filter the selection priority or change the type of face (e.g., planar, slab, shaft hole), if required.

   - The order in which tolerance features are added to the model should be carefully considered as this defines the datum identifiers (i.e, A, B, C) that are subsequently referenced. For example, primary Datum A is generally your primary mounting point/face for constraining the model. Datum B is the secondary reference for constraining, etc.

3. Click ✓. A preview of the GD&T appears
4. The annotation plane defines the plane on which the GD&T annotation is placed. If the default annotation plane does not display as required, consider using the following options:

   - Press <Space Bar> or right-click and select **Select Next Candidate Plane** to toggle between the default options, if available.

   - Press <Shift> or right-click and select **Select Annotation Plane** to select a specific plane.

The tools for selecting the annotation plane and the alignment options are the same as those used for the annotations discussed in Chapter 2.

5. (Optional) Once the annotation plane is active, and prior to selecting a placement location you can access options to align the annotation to existing references.

- Right-click, select **Align to Geometry**, and then select an edge or work axis. This alignment is temporary and if you move the cursor, the alignment is lost. Select in the graphics window to locate the annotation.

- Right-click and select **Toggle Alignment** to flip the orientation of the annotation, as shown in Figure 3–2.

The orientation of the annotation can be flipped using the Toggle Alignment option.

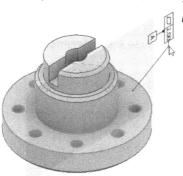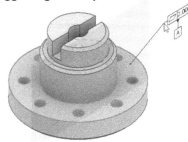

Figure 3–2

6. Select a location to place the annotation on the annotation plane. The mini-toolbar displays as shown in Figure 3–3. This mini-toolbar provides additional options to fully define the GD&T annotation.

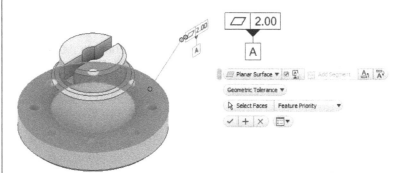

Figure 3–3

7. Use the mini-toolbars that display with the GD&T annotation preview to fully define it. The options available are dependent on the reference face that is selected. Figure 3–4 and Figure 3–5 show available options and how they can be used. Figure 3–5 only shows the tools that were not previously described in Figure 3–4. The goal of these images is to show you how to access the tools available for selection. It does not cover all scenarios.

Planar Surface

Select the tolerance type symbol in the feature control frame and use the mini-toolbar to change the tolerance scheme. The preferred option is marked with *. The available options are dependent on the feature selected. Additional datum reference features (DRF) can also be added when applicable.

Select the tolerance value and use the mini-toolbar to edit the value for the tolerance. Depending on the feature type, this mini-toolbar might contain options to define the material condition modifier.

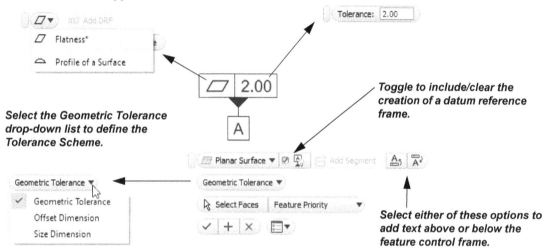

Select the Geometric Tolerance drop-down list to define the Tolerance Scheme.

Toggle to include/clear the creation of a datum reference frame.

Select either of these options to add text above or below the feature control frame.

Slab Surface

Select the tolerance value and use the mini-toolbar to edit the value for the tolerance or change its precision.

Select the slab thickness value and use the mini-toolbar to assign the tolerance type and precision.

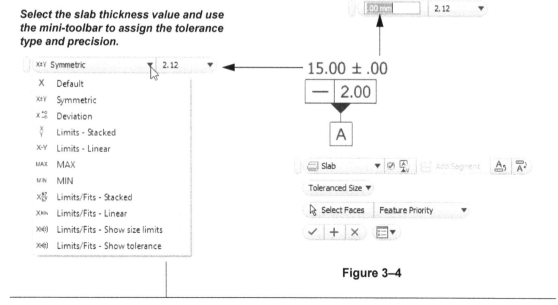

Figure 3–4

Hole Reference

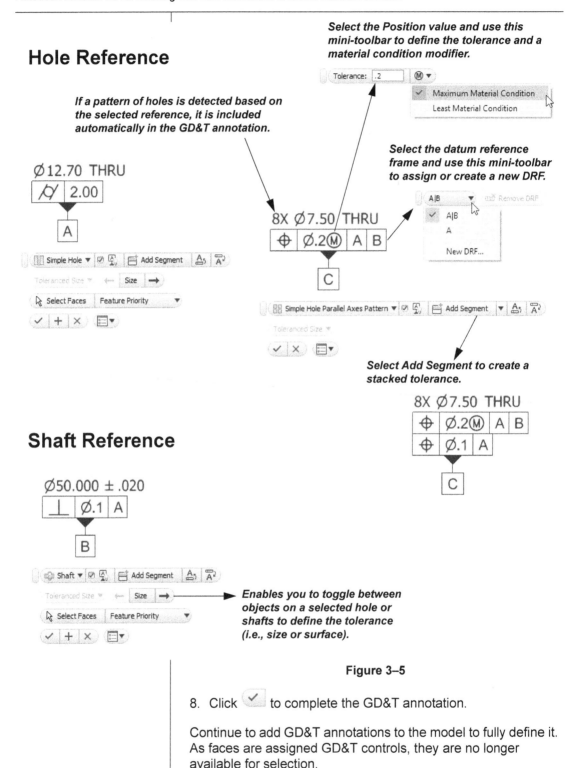

If a pattern of holes is detected based on the selected reference, it is included automatically in the GD&T annotation.

Select the Position value and use this mini-toolbar to define the tolerance and a material condition modifier.

Select the datum reference frame and use this mini-toolbar to assign or create a new DRF.

Select Add Segment to create a stacked tolerance.

Shaft Reference

Enables you to toggle between objects on a selected hole or shafts to define the tolerance (i.e., size or surface).

Figure 3–5

8. Click ✓ to complete the GD&T annotation.

Continue to add GD&T annotations to the model to fully define it. As faces are assigned GD&T controls, they are no longer available for selection.

Understanding the Tolerance Features Folder

All tolerance features are listed in the **Tolerance Features** folder in the Model Browser. Once the tolerance feature is expanded, it lists its feature control frame, datum identifier, dimensions, and reference geometry, as shown and described in Figure 3–6.

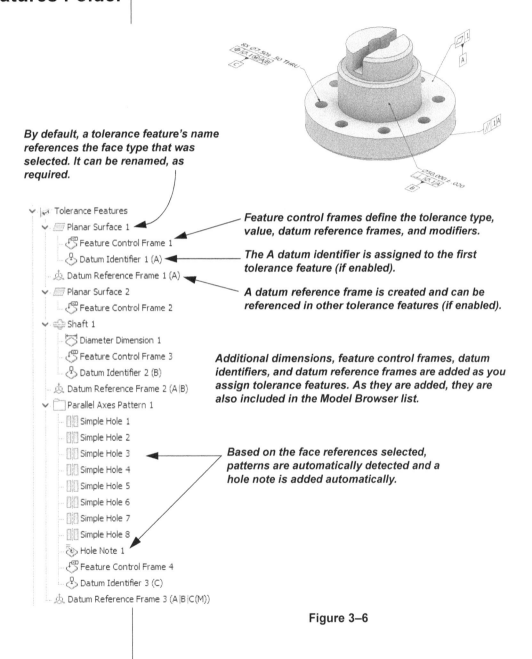

By default, a tolerance feature's name references the face type that was selected. It can be renamed, as required.

Feature control frames define the tolerance type, value, datum reference frames, and modifiers.

The A datum identifier is assigned to the first tolerance feature (if enabled).

A datum reference frame is created and can be referenced in other tolerance features (if enabled).

Additional dimensions, feature control frames, datum identifiers, and datum reference frames are added as you assign tolerance features. As they are added, they are also included in the Model Browser list.

Based on the face references selected, patterns are automatically detected and a hole note is added automatically.

Figure 3–6

Editing Tolerance Features

Once created, tolerance features display on the model and are listed in the **Tolerance Features** folder in the Model Browser. To edit, consider the following:

- Right-click on the tolerance feature annotation in the Model Browser or in the graphics window and select **Edit Tolerance Feature**. Alternatively, you can double-click on it. The same mini-toolbar used to create it displays for editing. Use any of the tools in the mini-toolbar to edit the tolerance feature.

- Right-click on a tolerance feature annotation in the Model Browser or in the graphics window and select any of the options displayed in its context menus. Figure 3–7 shows the context menus available for editing the tolerance feature (shown on left) and for editing the hole note associated with a tolerance feature (shown on right).

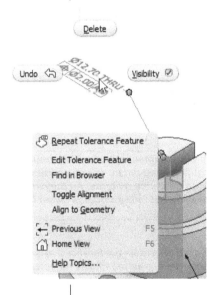
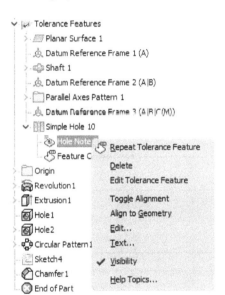

Figure 3–7

- Select a tolerance feature annotation in the Model Browser or in the graphics window to activate it. Select and drag the green circular reference at the elbow of the annotation (leader line/extension line) to change the location of the annotation on the circular edge.

- Select a tolerance feature annotation in the Model Browser or in the graphics window to activate it. Select the annotation text and drag it to change its location on the extension line.

- To delete a segment in a feature control frame or the feature control frame itself, select the tolerance type symbol and select **Remove Segment** or **Remove Feature Control Frame**, respectively. Figure 3–8 shows the mini-toolbars that become available when the tolerance type symbol is selected.

Figure 3–8

3.3 Datum Reference Frames

As tolerance features are assigned, datum identifiers can be automatically created as long as the option is enabled in the mini-toolbar. If enabled, the first tolerance feature creates Primary Datum A to define its placement face, the second creates the Secondary Datum B, and the third creates the Tertiary Datum C. Additionally, datum reference frames are also automatically created. As new tolerance features are created, they automatically reference the existing datum reference frames by assuming which should be used to describe the feature. Figure 3–9 shows that the datum reference frame A|B is used to define the position of patterned holes.

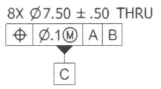

Figure 3–9

There are situations where the automatically defined datum reference frame might not correctly define a new tolerance feature. In these cases, you can assign an alternate or create a new one. This is done by selecting the datum reference frame area in the preview, as shown in Figure 3–10.

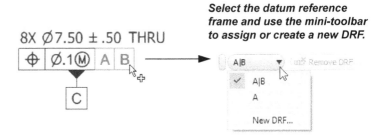

Select the datum reference frame and use the mini-toolbar to assign or create a new DRF.

Figure 3–10

How To: Create a Datum Reference Feature (DRF).

1. Use one of the following methods to create a DRF. In either case, the Datum Reference Frame dialog box opens.

   • In the *Annotate* tab>Geometric Annotation panel, click

    (DRF).

- In the feature control frame's preview, select the default datum reference frame to activate the mini-toolbar, (shown in Figure 3–10) and click **New DRF**.

2. Select a Primary, Secondary, and Tertiary datum reference from their respective drop-down lists to create the new datum reference frame.
3. Set the modifiers, as required.
4. Click **OK** to complete the datum reference frame. It is added to the **Tolerance Features** folder in the Model Browser.

Figure 3–11 shows the Datum Reference Frame dialog box set to create $\boxed{A \mid C \textcircled{M}}$. This datum reference frame can be used to define future tolerance features.

Figure 3–11

Editing a DRF

To edit a DRF, right-click on its name in the Model Browser and select **Edit DRF**. Alternatively, you can double-click on its name. The Datum Reference Frame dialog box opens. Manipulate the Primary, Secondary, Tertiary or Material Condition selections as required and click **OK**. If a DRF is being referenced by a tolerance feature, it will also update to reflect the change.

3.4 Tolerance Advisor

Tolerance features are used to accurately define the 3D model for manufacturing through the use of dimensions, geometric symbols, and tolerance values (GD&T's). As tolerance features are added in an Inventor model, the Tolerance Advisor tool is constantly evaluating what has been added and displays messages and warnings. The Tolerance Advisor displays as a Browser pane adjacent to the Model Browser. Figure 3–12 shows a model with seven tolerance features and its associated Tolerance Advisor Browser.

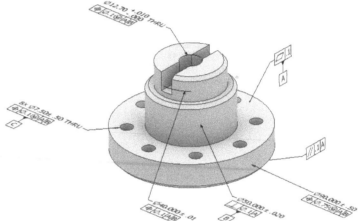

Figure 3–12

The Tolerance Advisor only evaluates tolerance feature and general profile note annotations.

The Tolerance Advisor helps guide you with the GD&T annotation of your model. The messages and warnings can be simply informational or can suggest missing information that should be included. The symbols adjacent to the messages and warnings help to classify them. As additional tolerance features are added, the information in the Tolerance Advisor updates. It is recommended that you review the messages and warnings as you annotate your model, to easily deal with the information as it is presented. Once fully annotated, you might still have messages displaying in the Tolerance Advisor that do not adversely affect the model.

To better understand the information or warnings in the model, double-click on the message to launch Autodesk Help. A description of the error along with possible resolutions are included, similar to that shown in Figure 3–13. Note that not all warnings may require a resolution. Use your knowledge of GD&T to correctly annotate your model.

Tolerance specification is incomplete

This message means that one of the following conditions exists in the model:

- A required tolerance value is zero or missing for a tolerance annotation.
- The Tolerance Zone Material Condition Modifier for a geometric tolerance has not been specified but is required. For example, for a position tolerance.

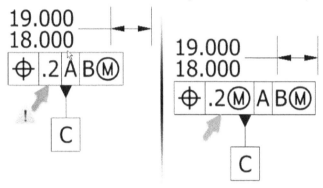

To resolve the issue, add the missing tolerance or modifier.

Figure 3–13

The Tolerance Advisor opens automatically when creating a tolerance feature. You can also open it from the *Annotate* tab>

Geometric Annotation panel, by clicking (Tolerance Advisor). To close it, select the option a second time or click **X**.

3.5 General Profile Note

If a general note annotation already exists in a quadrant, the general profile note is included with it.

A general profile note annotation can be used to assign a profile tolerance for faces that do not explicitly have a tolerance feature assigned. Only a single general profile note annotation can be assigned per model. Similar to a general note annotation, the general profile note annotation can only be added in one of the four quadrants of the graphics window. Figure 3–14 shows an example of a general profile note annotation added in the top-left quadrant (quadrant 2).

UNLESS OTHERWISE SPECIFIED, △.50 APPLIES TO ALL SURFACES

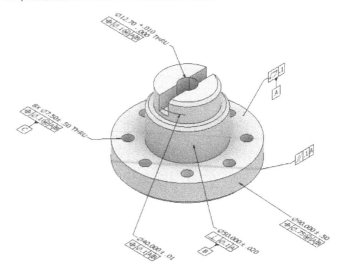

Figure 3–14

How To: Create a General Profile Note Annotation.

1. In the *Annotate* tab>Notes panel, click △.01 (General Profile Note).
2. Select one of the four quadrants around the graphics window to place the annotation. Once selected, the default text for the annotation displays in the graphics window.
3. Use the Format Text dialog box to modify the text associated with general profile note. Allowable modifications include:
   - Add additional text, or replace existing text, as required. The text can be modified before or after the **<<$GENERAL_PROFILE_TOL>>** parameter entry.
   - Change the font type, size, as well as any character customization (e.g., bold, italic, underline), as required.

The annotation scale does not control the size of the text. It must be set in the Format Text dialog box.

4. A default tolerance value is assigned to the annotation. To modify it, select the **<<$GENERAL_PROFILE_TOL>>** parameter in the Format Text dialog box, click 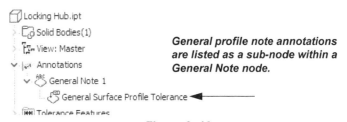, and enter a new value in the General Surface Profile Tolerance dialog box, as shown in Figure 3–15.

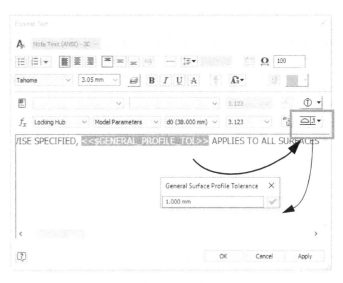

Figure 3–15

Once a general profile note annotation is added, the option is unavailable because only one is required per model.

5. Click **OK** to complete the general profile note annotation. Once added, it is listed in the **Annotations** folder in the Model Browser, as shown in Figure 3–16.

Locking Hub.ipt
> Solid Bodies(1)
> View: Master
∨ Annotations
   ∨ General Note 1
      General Surface Profile Tolerance ◄───────
> Tolerance Features

General profile note annotations are listed as a sub-node within a General Note node.

Figure 3–16

Editing a General Profile Note Annotation

The location of a general profile note cannot be modified once it is placed. You will have to delete and recreate it to place it in another quadrant. To edit the text of the note, in the **Annotations** folder, right-click on the **General Note** node to which it is associated, and select **Edit**. Alternatively, you can double-click on it. All edits are done using the same Format Text dialog box that was used to create it. If a general note annotation exists in the same quadrant, they will also be visible in the dialog box.

Practice 3a | Adding GD&T Annotations

Practice Objectives

- Create GD&T annotations in a model using the Tolerance Feature option.
- Create a general profile note annotation.
- Use the Tolerance Advisor to provide guidance on whether the model is correctly annotated.

In this practice, you will create the GD&T annotations shown in Figure 3–17 using tolerance features. Additionally, you will add the general profile note. As you progress through the practice, you will learn how to create the annotations and make edits to them.

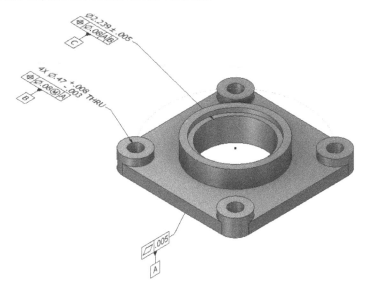

Figure 3–17

Task 1 - Review the active standard.

In this task, you will review the current Active Standard to ensure that it is set to **ASME**.

1. Open **Flange_Bearing.ipt**.

2. In the *Tools* tab>Options panel, click  (Document Settings). In the Document Settings dialog box, select the *Standard* tab and note that the Active Standard (as shown in Figure 3–18) is set as **ASME**. This standard was preset because the 2018 Imperial part standard template was used to create the model.

The default setting for a model created with the 2018 Metric part standard template is **ASME-mm**.

Figure 3–18

3. Close the Document Settings dialog box without making a change to the Active Standard.

Task 2 - Create the first tolerance feature.

In this task, you will create the first tolerance feature in the model on the bottom face of the model. In doing so, you will generate datum identifier A. Additionally, you will assign a feature control frame that describes the flatness with a .005 tolerance zone.

1. Rotate the model similar to that shown in Figure 3–19 to easily view the bottom face.

2. In the *Annotate* tab>Geometric Annotation panel, click

   (Tolerance Feature).

3. Select the bottom face of the model geometry in the location shown in Figure 3–19. The location selected determines the placement of the leader.

4. Based on the face selection, the software may recognize it as a Slab. In the mini-toolbar, select **Planar Surface**, as shown in Figure 3–19, if not already set.

Select the bottom face in this approximate location.

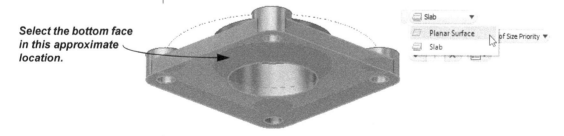

Figure 3–19

5. Click ✓. A preview of the GD&T displays.

6. Prior to selecting its placement location, press <Space Bar> to toggle the annotation plane to the one shown in Figure 3–20.

7. Select the placement location shown in Figure 3–20.

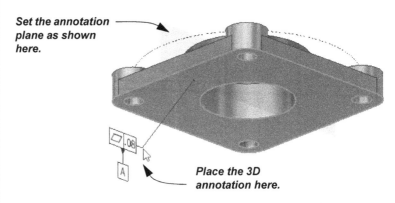

Set the annotation plane as shown here.

Place the 3D annotation here.

Figure 3–20

8. Once placed, a new mini-toolbar displays (as shown in Figure 3–21) to define the annotation.

- Datum identifier A was generated because the checkbox is enabled in the mini-toolbar and this tolerance feature was added first.
- The Flatness tolerance type was assigned.
- By default, a tolerance value of .08 was assigned.

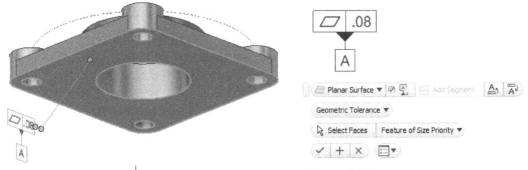

Figure 3–21

9. Select the **.08** tolerance value field in the mini-toolbar preview (not the actual GD&T preview). A new tolerance value mini-toolbar displays to enter a new value, as shown in Figure 3–22. Enter **.005** and press <Enter>.

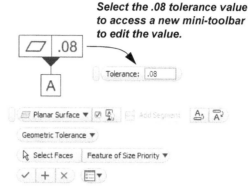

Figure 3–22

10. No additional changes are required. Click ✓ to complete the tolerance feature. The model and expanded **Tolerance Features** folder in the Model Browser display as shown in Figure 3–23. The tolerance feature contains:

- A feature control frame indicating the flatness and acceptable tolerance value for manufacturing.
- A datum identifier (A) attached to the feature control frame.
- A datum reference frame (A) was automatically generated with this tolerance feature and can be referenced in future annotations.

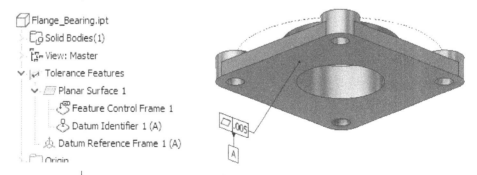

Figure 3–23

If the Tolerance Advisor doesn't open automatically, in the Annotate tab> Geometric Annotation panel, click 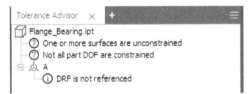 *(Tolerance Advisor).*

11. The Tolerance Advisor (shown in Figure 3–24) should open automatically now that a tolerance feature was created. The Tolerance Advisor indicates:

- Surfaces and part DOF remain unconstrained. This is because only one tolerance feature was added.

- The information message (ⓘ) highlights that DRF A is not yet referenced.

Tolerance Advisor × +

Flange_Bearing.ipt
- ⓘ One or more surfaces are unconstrained
- ⓘ Not all part DOF are constrained
- ⓐ A
  - ⓘ DRF is not referenced

Figure 3–24

Task 3 - Create a second tolerance feature.

In this task, you will create the second tolerance feature in the model and generate datum identifier B. The feature control frame generated defines the position of the pattern of bolt holes with respect to datum A.

1. Return the model to its default Home view.

2. In the *Annotate* tab>Geometric Annotation panel, click  (Tolerance Feature).

3. Select the inner cylindrical face of the bolt hole shown in Figure 3–25. The software may recognize it as a Simple Hole. Select the drop-down list and select **Simple Hole Parallel Axes Pattern**, if not already set.

Select this face to define the second tolerance feature.

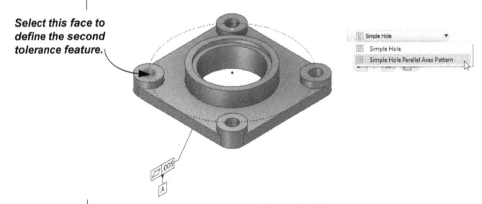

Figure 3–25

4. Click ✓. A preview of the GD&T appears.

5. Accept the default annotation plane and select the placement location shown in Figure 3–26.

6. Once placed, a new mini-toolbar displays (as shown in Figure 3–26) to define the annotation.

   • Datum identifier B was generated because the checkbox is enabled in the mini-toolbar and this feature is the second tolerance feature added.
   • A default positional tolerance type was assigned.
   • By default, the tolerance value for the position of the hole is **Ø.08**.
   • There are four thru holes (4X) with diameters of **Ø.47**.

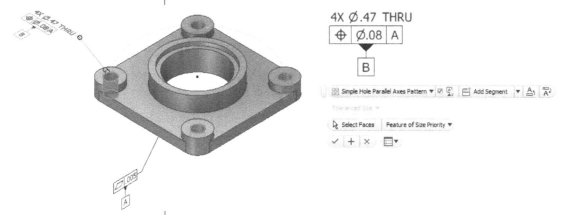

Figure 3–26

7. In the feature control frame, select the **Ø.08** tolerance value field in the mini-toolbar preview. A new mini-toolbar displays.

8. Maintain the default tolerance value, but expand the Material Condition drop-down list and select **Maximum Material Condition**, as shown in Figure 3–27.

Figure 3–27

9. Press <Enter> to close the mini-toolbar.

10. A Tolerance of + .008 and -.003 is required for the hole diameters. Select the **Ø.47** dimension value field above the feature control frame, in the mini-toolbar preview. A new mini-toolbar displays, as shown in Figure 3–28.

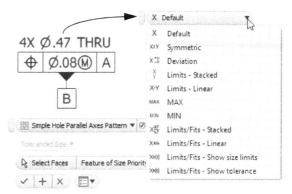

Figure 3–28

11. In the type list, select **Deviation**.

12. Select the top deviation value and enter **.008** as its new value, as shown in Figure 3–29. Press <Enter>.

13. Select the bottom deviation value and enter **-.003** as its new value, as shown in Figure 3–30. Press <Enter>.

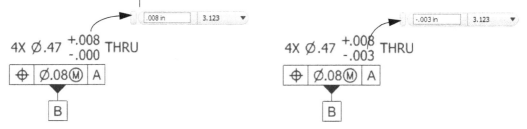

Figure 3–29   Figure 3–30

14. No additional changes are required. Click ✓. The model and expanded **Tolerance Features** folder displays as shown in Figure 3–31. The tolerance feature contains:

   - A feature control frame indicating the importance of the hole's position and its acceptable tolerance value for manufacturing.
   - A datum identifier that is attached to the feature control frame (B).
   - A datum reference frame (A|B(M)) was automatically generated with this tolerance feature and can be referenced in future annotations.

- A hole note indicating the number of holes, their diameter, and the acceptable tolerance for the hole diameter.

Flange_Bearing.ipt
> Solid Bodies(1)
> View: Master
∨ Tolerance Features
  > Planar Surface 1
    Datum Reference Frame 1 (A)
  ∨ Parallel Axes Pattern 1
    Simple Hole 1
    Simple Hole 2
    Simple Hole 3
    Simple Hole 4
    Hole Note 1
    Feature Control Frame 2
    Datum Identifier 2 (B)
  Datum Reference Frame 2 (A|B(M))
> Origin

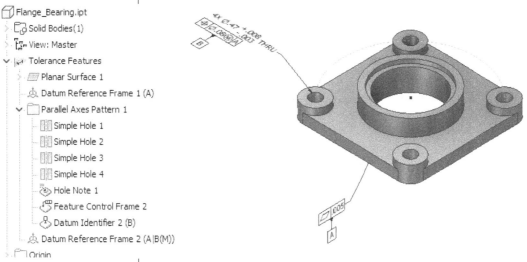

Figure 3–31

15. The Tolerance Advisor Browser updates as shown in Figure 3–32. The information in the Tolerance Advisor indicates:

- One of more surfaces remain unconstrained.

- The informational message ( ) highlights that DRF A|B(M) is not yet referenced.

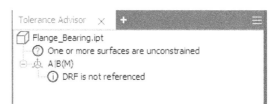

Figure 3–32

Task 4 - Create a third tolerance feature.

In this task, you will create a third tolerance feature in the model and generate datum identifier C. This feature control frame defines the position of the central hole.

1. In the *Annotate* tab>Geometric Annotation panel, click

   (Tolerance Feature).

2. Select the large inner cylindrical face of the model geometry as shown in Figure 3–33. Based on the face selection, the software recognizes it as a Simple Hole.

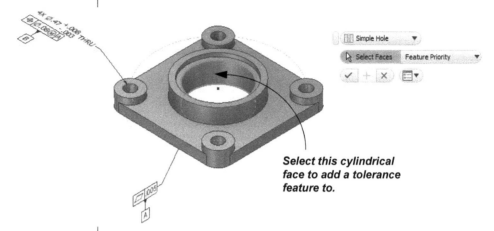

Figure 3–33

3. No changes are required. Click ✓.

4. Accept the annotation plane and select the placement location shown in Figure 3–34. The default GD&T does not accurately define the feature. Changes are required.

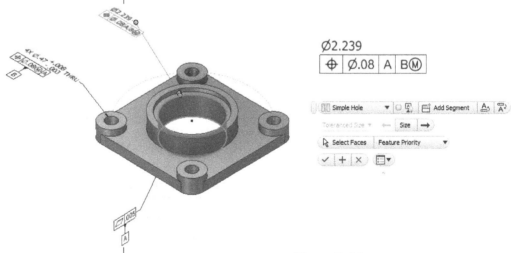

Figure 3–34

5. In the mini-toolbar, select ⬚🔲 to ensure that datum identifier C is added to the annotation.

6. Select the **Ø2.239** dimension value field above the feature control frame and expand the tolerance type list, as shown in Figure 3–35.

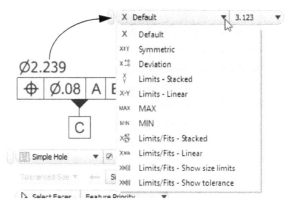

Figure 3–35

7. Select **Symmetric** and press <Enter>.

8. Select the **.000** tolerance value field shown in Figure 3–36 to open the new mini-toolbar. Enter **.005** as the new tolerance value. Press <Enter>.

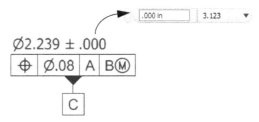

Figure 3–36

9. In the feature control frame, select the ⊕ tolerance type symbol.

10. In the mini-toolbar that becomes available, expand the Tolerance Type drop-down list and note that there is a list of available types that you can select from. The list only displays the types that you can use. Leave ⊕ as the selected type and press <Enter>.

11. A tolerance value of Ø.08 is acceptable. No changes are required for this value.

12. The datum reference frame A|B(M) is referenced automatically, as this frame was previously created for the patterned holes. The reference to the maximum material condition is not required. To redefine, select the datum reference frame field shown in Figure 3–37, and in the mini-toolbar select **New DRF**.

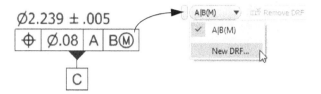

Figure 3–37

13. In the Datum Reference Frame dialog box, select **A** in the Primary drop-down list and **B** in the Secondary drop-down list, as shown in Figure 3–38. Click **OK**.

Figure 3–38

14. Click ✓ to complete the tolerance feature. The model and the expanded **Tolerance Features** folder in the Model Browser display as shown in Figure 3–39. The tolerance feature contains:

- A datum identifier (C) that is attached to the feature control frame.
- A feature control frame indicating the hole's acceptable positional tolerance value for manufacturing.
- A datum reference frame (C) that can be referenced in future annotations.
- The diameter size of the hole and its allowable tolerance value.

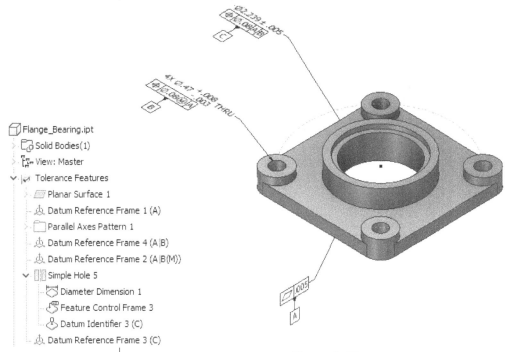

Flange_Bearing.ipt
- Solid Bodies(1)
- View: Master
- Tolerance Features
  - Planar Surface 1
  - Datum Reference Frame 1 (A)
  - Parallel Axes Pattern 1
  - Datum Reference Frame 4 (A|B)
  - Datum Reference Frame 2 (A|B(M))
  - Simple Hole 5
    - Diameter Dimension 1
    - Feature Control Frame 3
    - Datum Identifier 3 (C)
  - Datum Reference Frame 3 (C)

Figure 3–39

15. The Tolerance Advisor should update as shown in Figure 3–40. The information in the Tolerance Advisor indicates:

- One of more surfaces remain unconstrained.

- The informational messages (ⓘ) highlight that DRF A|B(M) and C are not yet referenced.

- The warning message (⚠) indicates that the tolerance specification for feature control frame 3 is incomplete.

Figure 3–40

16. In the Tolerance Advisor, double-click on the ⚠ **Tolerance specification is incomplete** message. The Help documentation opens as shown in Figure 3–41. Read the information on the warning and note that to resolve it, a modifier is required. Close the window and return to Inventor.

Tolerance specification is incomplete

This message means that one of the following conditions exists in the model:

- A required tolerance value is zero or missing for a tolerance annotation.
- The Tolerance Zone Material Condition Modifier for a geometric tolerance has not been specified but is required. For example, for a position tolerance.

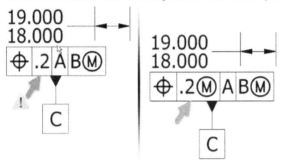

To resolve the issue, add the missing tolerance or modifier.

Figure 3–41

17. Double-click on **Feature Control Frame 3** to edit it.

18. In the feature control frame, select the **Ø.08** tolerance value field in the mini-toolbar preview. Maintain the default tolerance value but expand the Material Condition drop-down list and select **Maximum Material Condition**, as shown in Figure 3–42.

Figure 3–42

19. Complete the edit and note that the Tolerance Advisor no longer shows the warning.

Task 5 - Create a general profile note annotation.

In this task, you will add a general profile note annotation to indicate the profile tolerance value for all surfaces that are not explicitly annotated.

1. In the *Annotate* tab>Notes panel, click 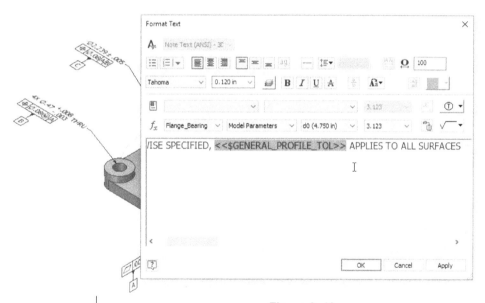 (General Profile Note).

2. Select the top-left quadrant (quadrant 2) in the graphics window to place the annotation. Once selected, the default text for the annotation and the Format Text dialog box display in the graphics window, as shown in Figure 3–43.

UNLESS OTHERWISE SPECIFIED, ⌓.04 APPLIES TO ALL SURFACES

Figure 3–43

3. The only change that is required for the default note is its tolerance value. Select **<<$GENERAL_PROFILE_TOL>>** in the Format Text dialog box and click ⌓.1▾.

The General Surface Profile dialog box is small and may open away from the Format Text dialog box.

4. Enter **0.05** in the General Surface Profile Tolerance dialog box, as shown in Figure 3–44. Then, click ✓.

Figure 3–44

5. Click **OK** to complete the general profile note annotation. It is listed in the **Annotations** folder in the Model Browser.

6. The Tolerance Advisor should update as shown in Figure 3–45. The information in the Tolerance Advisor indicates:

   - The informational messages (ⓘ) highlight that DRF A|B(M) and C are not yet referenced. This message is only informational and does not affect the model.
   - Note that no surfaces remain unconstrained now that the general profile note annotation was added.

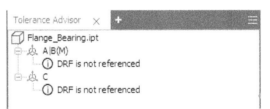

Figure 3–45

7. Save the model.

Chapter Review Questions

1. The order in which tolerance features are added to the model geometry affects which datum identifier names are added.

   a. True

   b. False

2. Which international GD&T standard governs how annotations should be added to a model to clearly describe its intent?

   a. ASME Y14.41

   b. ASME Y14.5M-1994

3. Which of the following context menu options enable you to select your own annotation plane to place a tolerance feature, as opposed to using the default options?

   a. Toggle Alignment

   b. Align to Geometry

   c. Select Next Candidate Plane

   d. Select Annotate Plane

4. Which of the following best describes how the datum reference frame A (shown in Figure 3–46) is created?

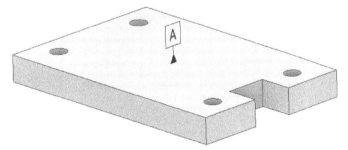

Figure 3–46

   a. Add a tolerance feature to the top face and remove its feature control frame during creation.

   b. Add a tolerance feature to the top face and clear its feature control frame's visibility once it has been created.

   c. Use the DRF option and select the top face.

5. Which of the following areas of the previewed tolerance feature annotation (shown in Figure 3–47) should be selected to assign a symmetric dimension tolerance?

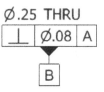

Figure 3–47

a. Ø.25

b. THRU

c. ⊥

d. Ø.08

e. A

f. B

6. Which of the following two tolerance features defines a Slab?

a.

15.000 ± .100

b.

7. Which of the following statements accurately describe the tolerance features shown in Figure 3–48? (Select all that apply.)

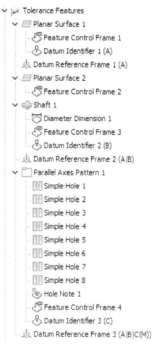

Figure 3–48

a. The three datum reference frames were created manually using the **DRF** option.

b. The selection of Planar Surface 2 did not generate a new datum identifier.

c. A single hole was selected and its entire pattern was identified and described in feature control frame 3.

d. There are three datum identifiers in the model.

8. The Tolerance Advisor is a tool used with the **Tolerance Feature** command to recommend the GD&T annotations that are required to fully describe a model.

a. True

b. False

9. Which of the following statements best describes how a general profile note annotation is located in a 3D model?

   a. Attached to a selected face.

   b. Attached to a selected edge.

   c. Attached to a selected point.

   d. Attached to a selected quadrant.

10. In which of the following two Model Browser folders is a general profile note annotation included once added to a 3D model?

   a. Annotations

   b. Tolerance Features

Command Summary

Button	Command	Location
	DRF (Datum Reference Frame)	• **Ribbon:** *Annotate* tab>Geometric Annotation panel • **Mini-toolbar:** during assignment of the datum reference frame for a Tolerance Feature
NA	**Edit (edit general profile note)**	• **Context Menu:** in Model Browser with General Profile Note selected
NA	**Edit DRF**	• **Context Menu:** in Model Browser with the DRF selected
NA	**Edit Tolerance Feature**	• **Context Menu:** in Model Browser with Tolerance Feature selected • **Context Menu:** in Graphics Window with Tolerance Feature selected
	General Profile Note	• **Ribbon:** *Annotate* tab>Notes panel
	Tolerance Advisor	• **Ribbon:** *Annotate* tab>Geometric Annotation panel
	Tolerance Feature	• **Ribbon:** *Annotate* tab>Geometric Annotation panel

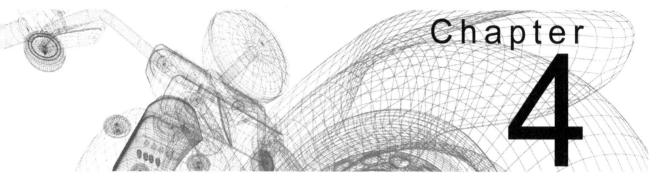

Chapter 4

Sharing 3D Annotations

In this chapter, you learn about the tools available in the Autodesk® Inventor® software that enable you to share your annotated 3D models so that they can be viewed as a 3D PDF or be read by other software applications. In this chapter, you also review other standard tools that enable you to create and manipulate the display of 3D annotations ensuring that the data is accurately shared. Additionally, you learn how to display 3D annotations in 2D drawing views.

Learning Objectives in this Chapter

- Work with Design Views in a model to accurately present the 3D annotations.
- Set the annotation scale for Design Views.
- Export your annotated model as a 3D PDF or as a STEP 242 file.
- Retrieve 3D model annotations into a 2D drawing view.

4.1 Displaying 3D Annotations

The final display or presentation of the PMI data is important regardless of how users will be consuming this data. The display of 3D annotations can be controlled using any of the following techniques:

- Manipulating the Design Views in the 3D model. These views can be customized to specified orientations and can be independently set to display specific annotations that have been created using visibility settings.

- Setting unique Annotation Scale values for Design Views.

Annotation Visibility

Design Views are discussed later in this section.

The visibility of 3D annotations can be controlled independently or globally for each Design View. Visibility can be controlled using the following options:

- Right-click on the **Annotations** or **Tolerance Features** folders in the Model Browser and select **Hide All Annotations**. Once any or all annotations are cleared, the **Show All Annotations** option becomes available in the context menu.

- Right-click on an annotation in the graphics window or its name in the Model Browser and clear the **Visibility** option to remove it from the display. To return it to the display, enable the option.

- The **3D Annotations** option in the Object Visibility drop-down list (*View* tab>Visibility panel) (shown in Figure 4–1) can also be used to clear all 3D annotations at once. This option does not individually toggle on or off 3D annotations.

Figure 4–1

Design Views

The process of creating Design Views for displaying PMI data is similar to how Design Views are used when modeling 3D geometry. They are used to save a specific view orientation and can include part color, work feature and sketch visibility, section views, and zoom level. In the case of 3D annotations, Design Views can control the visibility of annotations in specific views. These custom views are provided when exported to 3D PDF, providing an easy way to view the required annotations.

The default part templates that are provided in Autodesk Inventor include a **Master**, **Isometric**, and three planar (**Front**, **Top**, and **Right**) Design Views, as shown in Figure 4–2.

As of Autodesk Inventor 2017, models created with a default template contain four default Design Views. For models created prior to 2017, only a single Master Design View is provided in the default template.

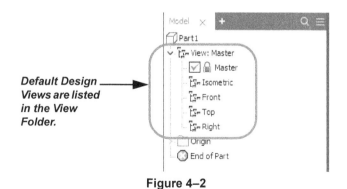

Figure 4–2

How To: Create a Design View for Use with 3D Annotations

1. Activate an existing Design View or create a new one.
   - To activate an existing view, right-click on its name and select **Activate** or double-click on it.

   New Design Views can be renamed by slowly double-clicking on their name and entering a descriptive name.

   - Right-click on the **View** node and select **New**, as shown in Figure 4–3. When a new view is created, it is automatically set to be active.

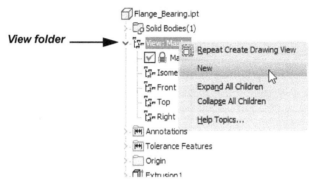

Figure 4–3

2. Control the annotation scale for the Design View.

   Annotation scales are described later in this topic.

3. Configure the view display (e.g., change the part and annotation orientation, toggle off the visibility of work features, sketches, or annotations).
4. (Optional) To lock a design view, right-click on the view name in the Model Browser and select **Lock**. Locking restricts you or others from making changes. Additionally, any changes made to the **Master** are not updated in a locked view.

To display an alternate Design View, right-click on its name in the Model Browser and select **Activate**. Alternatively, you can double-click on its name.

Hint: Working with Section Views

Incorporating Section Views within Design Views can help visualize a 3D model and its annotations by providing a section view of it. Prior to sectioning the model, the Design View to which it will be saved must be active. Additionally, any planes required to create the Section View must exist. You can select the type of section view in either the *Annotate* or *View* tab. Refer to the *Inventor Introduction to Solid Modeling* learning guide for more information on how to create a Section View or refer to the Inventor Help documentation.

Annotation Scale

The scale of the annotations that are created using the annotation tools are automatically set based on the model size. The automatic scale value is shown in the drop-down list in the Manage panel, as shown in Figure 4–4.

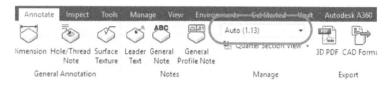

Figure 4–4

- The annotation scale for the Design Views listed in the **View** node are initially set using this automatic value.

The annotation scale cannot be changed for the Master Design View or any locked Design View.

- To assign a unique annotation scale, ensure that a Design View, other than the **Master**, is active. You can select a scale value from the list in the Manage panel or right-click on the Design View name in the Model Browser and select a value in the **Annotation Scale** menu. These options are shown in Figure 4–5.

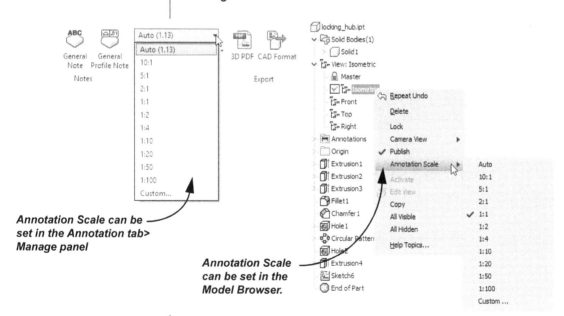

Annotation Scale can be set in the Annotation tab> Manage panel

Annotation Scale can be set in the Model Browser.

Figure 4–5

- If the model geometry changes affecting the size of the model, any Design Views set to **Auto** automatically update to reflect the change. Design Views that have been assigned specific annotation values will not change.

4.2 Exporting 3D Annotations

The choice of export options that should be used to share your annotated 3D model is dependent on the following:

- If the 3D annotations were created for visual purposes, the model can be shared and viewed as a 3D PDF.

- If the 3D annotations were created in support of an MBD modeling environment where the export file format must be machine readable (i.e., CNC tools), the model can be shared as STEP 242 file format.

Additional export file formats are also available to export the 3D model geometry.

3D PDF

A 3D PDF is strictly graphical. This is intended to be readable for visual inspection and display by a user. The Anark 3D PDF Publishing add-in is automatically installed to support this export format. Figure 4–6 shows an example of a 3D PDF file.

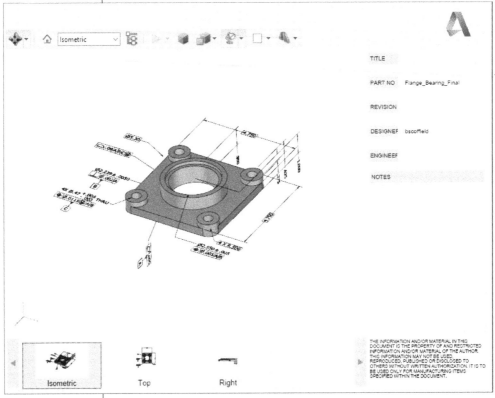

Figure 4–6

Prior to exporting the model as a 3D PDF, ensure that all the required Design Views are created and are set to display the required annotations. When exported, each Design View is exported and is provided for viewing within the PDF file.

How To: Create a 3D PDF

1. In the *Annotate* tab>Export panel, click  (3D PDF). Alternatively, you can also access this command by clicking **File>Export>3D PDF**. The Publish 3D PDF dialog box opens as shown in Figure 4–7.

Figure 4–7

2. In the *Properties* area, select which properties are to be added to the 3D PDF.
3. In the *Design View Representations* area, select which Design View include in the 3D PDF.
4. In the *Visualization Quality* area, select the quality that should be used to create the 3D PDF.
5. In the *Export Scope* area, select whether all entities are to be exported (**All Entities**) or if the data exported should be limited to that related in Design Views (**Limit to entities in the selected Design View Representations**).
6. (Optional) In the *Template* area, use the browse tool to assign a custom template for the 3D PDF. If no custom template is assigned, the default template is used.

7. In the *File Output Location*, select the location to which the new 3D PDF should be saved.
8. Clear or enable the **View PDF when finished** option, as required.
9. In the *Attachments* area, select to attach an exported STEP file at the same time. Additionally, you can attach supplemental attachments with the 3D PDF, if required.
10. Click **Publish** to create the 3D PDF.

If the **View PDF when finished** option was selected during creation, the 3D PDF will open immediately. Otherwise, locate the file and open it to view the PDF. To navigate in the 3D PDF, hover the cursor over the 3D model to access the Toolbar:

- Select a Design View name at the bottom of the 3D PDF to activate it or select a name in the drop-down list in the Toolbar.

- The expanded options shown in Figure 4–8 enable you to manipulate the model display. Additional options on this toolbar enable you to return to its Home View, change the perspective and rendering settings, control lights, and set the background color. If cross sections exist in a Design View, you can also control their display setting.

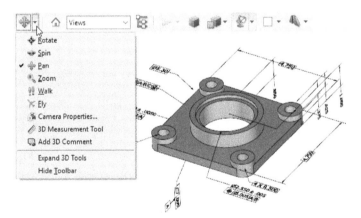

Figure 4–8

Adobe Acrobat Professional is required to manage and save new views.

- Once an existing view has been manipulated, you may want to save it for reuse. To create a new view in the 3D PDF, expand the Views drop-down list and select **Manage Views**. In the Manage Views dialog box, you can select which settings will be retained in the manipulated view.

If new views or changes are made to the 3D PDF save the file before closing so that the changes are maintained in the file.

STEP 242

Exporting an annotated 3D model using the STEP 242 file format provides a sharing format that is machine readable. This format enables software applications and CNC tools to directly use the annotations.

This file format is in support of an MBD modeling environment.

How To: Export to STEP 242

1. In the *Annotate* tab>Export panel, click ⬚ (CAD Format). Alternatively, you can also access this command by clicking **File>Export>CAD Format**. The Save As dialog box opens.
2. In the Save As type drop-down list, select **STEP Files**.
3. Click **Options**. The Options dialog box opens as shown in Figure 4–9.

Figure 4–9

4. In the *Application Protocol* area, select **242 - Managed Model Based 3D Engineering**.
5. Enter a *Spline Fit Accuracy* value or accept the default.
6. Select **Include Sketches** to ensure that sketch features are included in the output data.
7. In the remaining fields, enter information, as required.
8. Click **OK** to create the STEP 242 file for sharing.

4.3 3D Annotations in Drawings

When working in an MBD environment, adding 3D annotations eliminates the need to create 2D Drawings. If companies still require 2D drawings, a 3D model can still be annotated for viewing purposes (3D PDF) and the annotations can be retrieved into a drawing. If changes are made in the model, an associative link is maintained and the drawing updates.

How To: Retrieve 3D Annotations in Drawing Views.

1. Create a new drawing or open an existing one.
2. Place views in the drawing, as required.
3. Right-click on the view and select **Retrieve Model Annotations**, as shown in Figure 4–10. This option is available for either isometric or orthographic views.

Figure 4–10

4. In the Retrieve Model Annotation dialog box (shown in Figure 4–11), select the *3D Annotations* tab. A Design View is selected by default. Only the tolerance features and annotations that were set as visible for that Design View are visible in the drawing view. Change the Design View in the drop-down list, if required.

The view type (Isometric or Orthographic) displays in the name of the dialog box depending on the view that was selected.

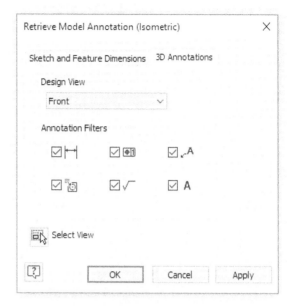

Figure 4–11

5. Refine the display of the annotations for the active Design View, as required.

   - Annotations can be selected directly in the preview to be added. If none are selected, they are all automatically added.

   - Enable/disable the annotation types in the Annotation Filters.

6. To change the view to which the annotations are being added, click ⊞ (Select View) and select a new view.

Consider using the Sketch and Feature Dimensions tab to retrieve these dimension types.

7. Click **OK** to add the previewed or selected annotations to the view and close the dialog box. To continue to add annotations to other views, click **Apply**.

Practice 4a

Sharing your Annotations

Practice Objectives

- Control the display of 3D annotations in Design Views.
- Lock a Design View so that changes made to the Master Design View do not affect the view.
- Export the annotated 3D model for sharing.
- Add 3D annotations in 2D drawing views.

In this practice, you will work with an existing model that has had annotations and tolerance features added. You will learn how to customize the Design Views that come predefined in the part template. By customizing these views, you are creating the views that will be exported or used in a 2D drawing view.

Task 1 - Manipulate the annotations displayed in the default Design Views.

By default, four Design Views exist in this model because it used the default part template when it was created. In this task, you will activate each Design View and manipulate how the annotations display. Once customized, you will also lock the Design View so that additional changes are not made inadvertently.

1. Open **Flange_Bearing_Final.ipt**.

2. Expand the **View** node in the Model Browser. All of the default Design Views are shown in Figure 4–12.

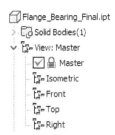

Figure 4–12

3. Right-click on the **Isometric** Design View and select **Activate**.

4. Select the *Annotate* tab. In the Manage panel, expand the Annotation Scale drop-down list and select **2:1**. This selection increases the display size of the annotations for this view.

5. Complete the following changes (similar to those shown in Figure 4–13) to the Design View:

- Change the zoom level on the model to fill the graphics window. Rotate the view, as required.
- Reposition annotations, as required.
- Select the material note, right-click and clear the **Visibility** option.
- Toggle the alignment of the **Planar Surface 1** tolerance feature, as well as its location.

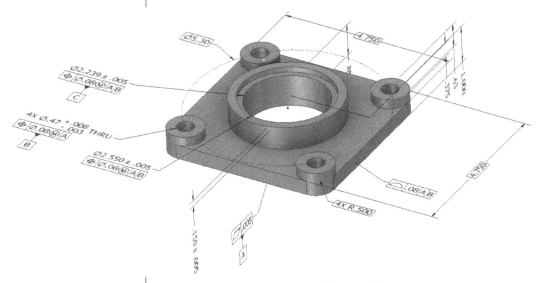

Figure 4–13

6. Expand the **Annotations** folder in the Model Browser and note that **Leader Text 1** displays as gray. This is the material annotation and it is no longer visible in this view.

7. Right-click on the **Isometric** Design View in the Model Browser and select **Lock**.

8. Right-click on the **Master** Design View and select **Activate**. Alternatively, you can double-click a view name to activate it.

9. The **Master** view always displays with the current view orientation and zoom. Return the model to its default Home View. Note the following:

- The annotation scale is still set to **Auto (1.58)**.
- The material note is still visible.

Any custom annotation scaling or visibility setting is not visible in the **Master** Design View.

10. Activate the **Isometric** Design View. Note that it displays based on the previous zoom, orientation, scale setting, and annotation visibility that were set when it was active. These settings are stored with the Design View so that it can be retrieved at any time.

> **TIP:** If additional annotations are added to the **Master** Design View, they will not be visible in the **Isometric** Design View because it has been locked and is set to prevent changes from affecting it.

11. Activate the **Top** Design View. The view displays similar to that shown in Figure 4–14

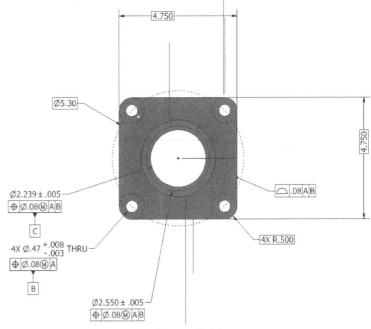

Figure 4–14

12. Expand the **Annotations** folder in the Model Browser, if not already expanded. Note that all the annotations display in black font, indicating they are all visible in this view.

13. Any of the annotations that are not planar with the **Top** view display as lines. Their display can be cleared to help clean-up the Design View. Right-click on the linear entity shown in Figure 4–15 and clear its **Visibility** option.

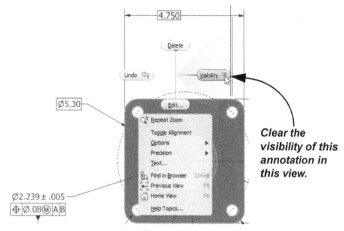

Clear the visibility of this annotation in this view.

Figure 4–15

You can use a combination of selecting annotations in the graphics window or in the Model Browser to clear them from the display. The choice is based on which is easier to select.

14. In the **Annotations** folder, note that the **Linear Dimension 6** annotation now displays with a gray font, indicating that it has been cleared from the display.

15. Locate other annotations that are not required in the **Top** Design View and clear them from the display. The **Annotations** and **Tolerance Features** folder, along with the view should display similar to that shown in Figure 4–16 once done. Move the 3D annotations, as required.

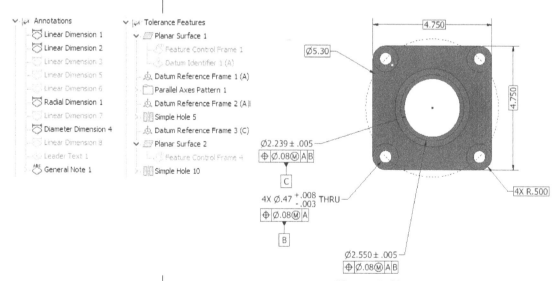

Figure 4–16

16. Right-click on the **Top** Design View in the Model Browser and select **Lock**.

17. Activate the **Right** Design View. The view should display similar to that shown in Figure 4–17.

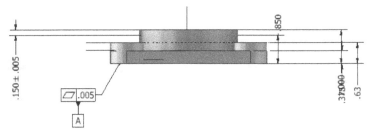

Figure 4–17

18. Complete the following in the **Right** Design View. The view should display similar to that shown Figure 4–18 once done.

- Right-click on the **Tolerance Features** folder name and select **Hide All Annotations**.
- Clear all but the four linear dimensions shown.
- Move the dimensions similar to that shown.
- Right-click on **Sketch6** at the bottom of the Model Browser and clear its visibility. This sketch consists of a single construction circle that was added to show the position of the circle of patterned holes.
- Change the precision of the dimensions, as required, so that they display as shown in Figure 4–18.

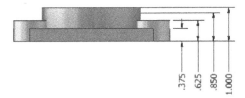

Figure 4–18

19. Right-click on the **Right** Design View in the Model Browser and select **Lock**.

20. Right-click on the **Front** view and select **Delete**. Because of the symmetric nature of this model no additional annotations are required and this view can be deleted from the model.

21. Save the model.

Task 2 - Export the model as a STEP 242 file.

In this task, you will learn to export an annotated 3D model as a STEP 242 file.

1. Activate the **Master** Design View and return to the default Home View on the ViewCube. Adjust the annotation placement, if required.

2. In the *Annotate* tab>Export panel, click ⬒ (CAD Format). Alternatively, you can also access this command by clicking **File>Export>CAD Format**. The Save As dialog box opens.

3. In the Save as type drop-down list, select **STEP Files**.

4. Click **Options**.

5. In the *Application Protocol* area, select **242 - Managed Model Based 3D Engineering**.

6. Accept the default value for *Spline Fit Accuracy*.

7. Select **Include Sketches** to ensure that sketch features are included.

8. Leave the remaining fields empty. Click **OK** and then click **Save** to create the STEP 242 file.

9. Navigate to the working directory and note that the new .STP file has been created.

Task 3 - Export the model as a 3D PDF file.

In this task, you will learn to export an annotated 3D model to a 3D PDF file. Once created, you will manipulate the file to review the annotations.

1. Return to Autodesk Inventor.

2. In the *Annotate* tab>Export panel, click 🄿 (3D PDF). As an alternative, you can also access this command by clicking **File>Export>3D PDF**. The Publish 3D PDF dialog box opens as shown in Figure 4–19.

As of the release of this learning guide (June 2017), Autodesk Inventor does not currently support the import of a Step 242 file format. Opening this file to review the annotations cannot be tested.

Figure 4–19

3. In the *Properties* and *Design View Representations* areas, maintain the default settings that include all properties and the three customized Design Views in the final PDF.

4. In the *Visualization Quality* area, select **Medium** quality from the drop-down list.

5. Ensure that the **Limit to entities in the selected Design View Representations** option is selected in the *Export Scope* area.

6. Maintain the default template and file output location. These settings store the file in the current working directory using the same file name as the model.

7. Ensure that the **View PDF when finished** option is selected.

8. No STEP file or attachments are currently required. Click **Publish** to create the 3D PDF.

9. Once opened, review the PDF. Each of the three Design Views are listed along the bottom of the file. Select each Design View individually to display them.

10. Activate the **Isometric** Design View. Hover the cursor over the model geometry and use the commands on the Toolbar to manipulate the display of the Isometric Design View.

11. Change the background color, render display, and set lights, as required.

12. In the *View* drop-down list select **Manage Views**. The Adobe Acrobat Professional software is required to manage and save new views in a 3D PDF. If you are using Adobe Reader, you will not be able to complete the next four steps.

13. Click **New View** and ensure that all *Display Settings* are enabled so that they are saved in the new view. Click **OK**.

14. Click **OK** to close the Manage Views dialog box.

15. **New 4** is added to the list of Managed Views. Switch back to one of the other views and note that the background and lights return to their default.

16. Save the PDF file.

17. Close the PDF file and return to Autodesk Inventor.

Task 4 - Retrieve 3D annotations into a drawing view.

In this task you will create a new Design View that contains only tolerance feature annotations. These annotations will be added to a 2D drawing view.

1. Right-click on the **View** node and select **New**.

2. Select the new view, click again (do not double-click) and enter [**GD&T only**] as the new name for the view.

3. Maintain the default Home View orientation and the default Annotation Scale for the view.

4. Right-click on the **Annotations** folder and select **Hide All Annotations**.

5. Toggle off the visibility of **Sketch6**.

6. Lock the new **GD&T only** Design View.

7. Save the model.

8. Open **Flange_Bearing_Final_Drawing.idw**.

9. Right-click on the **Isometric** view in the top right-hand corner of the drawing and click **Retrieve Model Annotations**.

10. Select the *3D Annotations* tab in the Retrieve Model Annotation dialog box.

11. Select **GD&T only** in the Design View drop-down list, if not already active. All of the annotation features display in this view.

12. Click **Apply** to add the 3D annotations to the view and leave the dialog box open to add additional 3D annotations.

13. Ensure that 🔲 (Select View) is active and select the bottom left-hand view shown in Figure 4–20.

14. If the Design View is not already changed to the **Top** Design View, select it in the drop-down list.

15. In the *Annotation Filters* area, clear all but the General Dimension filter (⊢⊣).

16. Click **OK** to finish retrieving annotations. Move the annotations as required. The drawing should display similar to that shown in Figure 4–20.

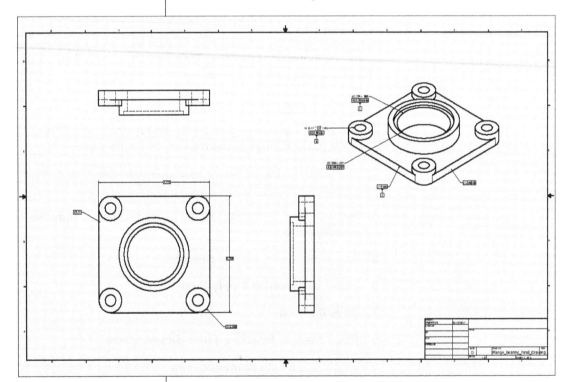

Figure 4–20

17. Save the drawing and the model. Close all files.

Chapter Review Questions

1. Which of the following are valid options for controlling the visibility of 3D annotations in a model? (Select all that apply.)

   a. Right-click on an annotation in the graphics window and clear the **Visibility** option.

   b. Right-click on an annotation in the Model Browser and clear the **Visibility** option.

   c. Right-click on the **Annotations** folder in the Model Browser and click **Hide All Annotations**.

   d. In the *View* tab>Visibility panel, clear the **3D Annotations** option.

2. Which of the following statements are true regarding the Annotation Scale used in a Design View. (Select all that apply.)

   a. The default annotation scale is based on the Active Standard that is set.

   b. The default annotation scale can be modified for all Design Views at once by selecting a new scale value in the Annotation Scale drop-down list (*Annotate* tab> Manage panel).

   c. The default annotation scale can be modified for a single Design View by right-clicking on its name in the Model Browser and selecting a new value in the **Annotation Scale** fly-out menu.

   d. Once a Design View is locked, the annotation scale cannot be modified unless the view is unlocked.

3. Part files created in an earlier software version that did not have predefined Design Views, cannot create new Design Views.

   a. True

   b. False

4. Which of the following customizations made to a model's display can be saved in a Design View? (Select all that apply.)

    a. Unique active standard for each Design View

    b. View orientation

    c. Zoom level

    d. Visibility of 3D annotations

    e. Sectioned views

5. Which export option is best used if an end-user intends to open the file on an iPad to sign off on its design?

    a. 3D PDF

    b. IGES

    c. STEP 242

    d. STL

6. Which export option is best used if the file is required for use on a CNC machine to accurately manufacture a component for use in the aerospace industry?

    a. 3D PDF

    b. IGES

    c. STEP 242

    d. STL

7. Which of the following are valid methods to customize which 3D annotations are to be shown in a 2D drawing view? (Select all that apply.)

    a. Set a Design View.

    b. Set the annotation filter options.

    c. Set the visibility of the annotations for each drawing view.

    d. Select the previewed annotations that are to be kept.

Command Summary

Button	Command	Location
N/A	**3D Annotations (Object Visibility)**	• **Ribbon:** *View* tab>Visibility panel, expanded Object Visibility drop-down list
N/A	**Annotation Scale**	• **Ribbon:** *Annotate* tab>Manage panel • **Context Menu:** in Model Browser with Design View name selected
N/A	**Hide All Annotations**	• **Context Menu:** in Model Browser with the Annotations or Tolerance Features folders selected
N/A	**New** (Design View)	• **Context Menu:** in Model Browser on View folder
N/A	**Retrieve Model Annotations**	• **Context Menu:** in graphics window with view selected
N/A	**Show All Annotations**	• **Context Menu:** in Model Browser with the Annotations or Tolerance Features folders selected
N/A	**Visibility**	• **Context Menu:** in Model Browser with the annotation name selected • **Context Menu:** in Graphics Window with the annotation selected

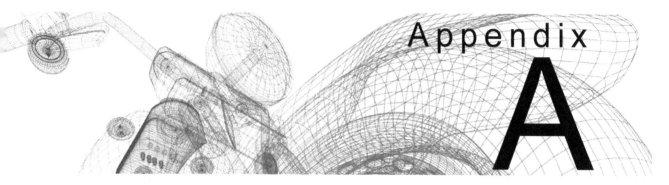

A

Additional Practices

This appendix provides additional practices that can be used to review 3D annotation functionality that was taught in this learning guide.

Practice A1 | Annotating 3D Models

Practice Objective

- Use the required 3D annotation features to annotate the models provided.

In this practice you are provided part models and are required to annotate them using the 3D annotation tools discussed in this learning guide. Minimal instruction is provided.

Task 1 - Add 3D annotations to a part model.

Light_Switch_Cover_Final.ipt has been included in the practice files for you to review, if required.

1. Open **Light_Switch_Cover.ipt**. Add the 3D annotations shown in Figure A–1. Consider the following tips:

   - The three dimensional annotations are Basic dimensions and are dimensioned to the centers of the fillets and holes.
   - The profile of surface tolerance feature references the four planar surfaces that surround the switch.
   - The overall length and width tolerance features reference planar faces on each end to measure slab thickness.

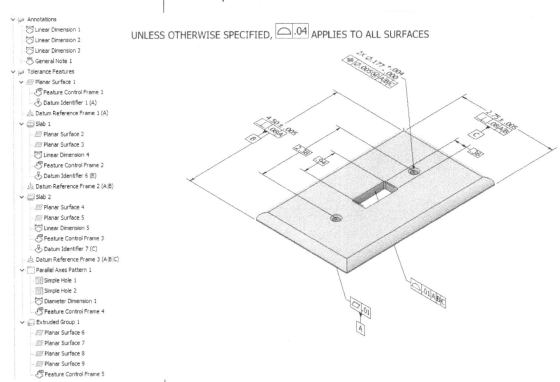

Figure A–1

2. Modify or create the Design Views as follows:

   - Set the **Isometric** Design View with a 1:1 annotation scale.

   - Modify each Design View so that only the planar annotations display in each view.

Task 2 - Add 3D annotations to part models and customize the Design Views.

---

*SkateBoard_Wheel_*
Final.ipt has been
included in the practice
files for you to review, if
required.

1. Open **SkateBoard_Wheel.ipt**. Use the annotation tools available on the *Annotate* tab to add the 3D annotations shown in Figure A–2. Consider the following tips:

   - Toggle on the visibility of the **XY Plane** and select it as the annotation plane for the four dimensional annotations and the two Planar Surface tolerance features.

   - Select the **Annotation Plane** work plane as the annotation plane for the Hole and Shaft tolerance features.

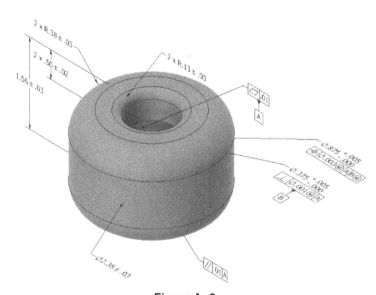

Figure A–2

2. Modify or create the Design Views as described below.

   - Set the **Isometric** Design View with a 1:1 annotation scale.

- Create an **Isometric_No_Annotations** Design View and hide all 3D annotations. Lock this Design View so that any new annotation is not included.
- Modify the **Front** Design View so that it is sectioned through the XY Plane and displays the annotations shown at the top of Figure A–3. Rename the Design View as **Front_Sectioned**.
- Modify the **Top** Design View so that it is sectioned through the Annotation Plane work plane and display the annotations shown in Figure A–3. Rename the Design View as **Top_Sectioned**.
- Delete the **Right Design** View.

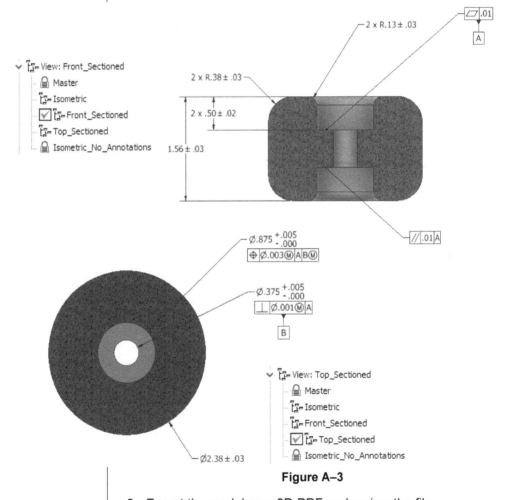

Figure A–3

3. Export the model as a 3D PDF and review the file.

4. Save and close the models.

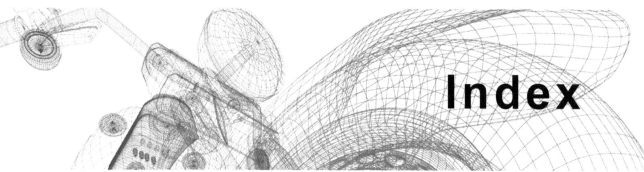

Index

www.ingramcontent.com/pod-product-compliance
Lightning Source LLC
Chambersburg PA
CBHW080421060326
40689CB00019B/4330